MASTERY AT WORK

18 Keys For Achieving Success, Fulfillment And Joy In Any Profession

By
Nicole Grace

MANI PRESS
SANTA FE

MASTERY AT WORK
Published by Mani Press
369 Montezuma Avenue, Suite 415
Santa Fe, NM 87501

Book cover design by Lightbourne and Kelly Harrison
Book layout by Fine Line Design

ISBN: 0-9747852-1-0

Library of Congress Control Number: 2004112235

TABLE OF CONTENTS

For Dr. Charles Wurtz

INTRODUCTION

On subways and in elevators, in buses and on the streets, faces of commuters tell the story of a culture of work rampant with boredom and despair. As we travel to and from our offices day after day, most of us look and feel miserable and defeated, like wild animals caged. Wanting freedom, craving peace, but not knowing how or where to find release, we drag ourselves back and forth from our places of employment in a tragedy of hopeless routine. Work does not have to be this empty. Life does not have to be this unfulfilling. In *Mastery At Work,* I will show you how to break free.

I discovered the techniques described in this book over time, from personal revelations as well as secret teachings. Like following breadcrumbs dropped along a path through the woods, I have retraced my steps on the journey in order to document the Keys for success, fulfillment and joy that I came upon by grace and that were transmitted to me along the way. These Keys will open the doors of potential for every individual, not just special, privileged or spiritually-oriented people. The techniques described here will work for you.

My journey began early on, when I first discovered that there are greater powers at work in this world than are commonly understood. Though most of my memories of childhood have been shrouded by the fog of time, this particular memory is visceral and clear. No more than a baby, I was planted in the sand behind a beach house my parents had rented in Amagansett, New York, playing with a red plastic shovel and blue pail. The sand felt warm underneath my legs, bare and splayed out from under my short, summer dress. Looking up, quite suddenly, my familiar world of house and car, sky and sand became filled with a bright, ethereal radiance. The mist-like effulgence began to obscure the outlines of the objects around me until everything I had been able to see a moment before dissolved into a magnificent ocean of golden light. Then, I dissolved into that light, into a womb of warm, glowing, ecstatic bliss.

During my fourteenth year my mother was in the hospital around the corner dying of cancer, and I had my second clear indication that science had not provided answers for all of life's unusual experiences. Sitting on my bed lamely attempting to study for my biology final, while images of my mother's bloated face welled up like tears, I felt a strange and powerful burst of energy rush through my body like a train. The vibration shivered from my feet up my spine and out the top of my head. I looked at the clock and noted the white digits of the time. Mystified, I turned back to the same paragraph I had attempted to read several times before. After about an hour, I heard the sound of many pairs of shoes clacking on the wooden floor of the foyer and voices whispering. Later I discovered that my mother had passed away at precisely the moment I had felt that strange rush of energy. Perhaps, I thought, my best friend and caretaker had come to say goodbye.

Thus was launched a lifelong search for Truth. I was fortunate to encounter gifted spiritual teachers in my seeking, who showed me specific tools saints have used throughout the ages to find meaning from the confusion of daily life. But it wasn't until I met a Himalayan master and became ordained as a Buddhist monk that I was able to identify and resolve what I felt was missing from my other instruction: the link between a spiritual life of experiencing exalted states of consciousness and the seemingly mundane and unenlightened world of work and business that filled all the hours in between formal morning and evening practice.

This teacher insisted on his students becoming successful professionals. Directed to emerge from the proverbial cave and find meaningful employment, I discovered the field of project management. I pursued this science as a strenuous mental discipline that could provide a financially viable career and yet also allow me to put into practice traditional spiritual ideals, such as compassion, discrimination and humility.

Finally I was able to bring into the banal exercises of commuting to and working in an office the peace and joy I had been able to touch while meditating or sitting in the presence of a master. It became clear that no search for peace, fulfillment, lasting joy or, ultimately, even success can be complete without joining professional discipline, ethics, etiquette and expertise to a personal striving for greatness.

Mastery At Work: 18 Keys For Achieving Success, Fulfillment And Joy In Any Profession presents a pathway for making one's life virtuous and accomplished. It is a practical prescription for excelling in the world of commerce and business, based on techniques for excelling individually in ways that can't be measured in dollar signs. I have named this philosophy The Three-Fold Path to Mastery: an enlightened approach to life and work. This book and the philosophy it describes propose that the majority of individuals cannot realistically attain significant personal growth without addressing growth at, and through, work. It is the practice and discipline of working impeccably that provides us with the necessary template for achieving personal evolution. At the same time, by striving to be a nobler, kinder, wiser human being we find the motivation for seeking perfection in our work. The equation is: work as spiritual practice and spiritual practice as work. Together we find a true pathway to mastery: Mastery At Work.

Rather than embracing a single religion or spiritual course, over the years I have searched for the common thread underlying them all. That, to me, is where we find Truth unadorned and uncorrupted by the specifics of any particular Way. The undercurrent of spirituality that you will find in *Mastery At Work* is not representative of any single path, but rather exists as a tapestry through which is woven the fundamental principles of many, including Buddhism, Zen, Hinduism, Vedanta, Qabalah and Mysticism.

Five years ago, towards the end of a consulting assignment far from my home facilitating the merger of two corporate giants, I experienced what could only be described as a calling. It was as if the universe herself were whispering in my ear, "Conclude your current project. Write a book." It was time for a change anyway and thankfully I listened to the call. The morning after I returned home I sat down to meditate, with the fall Hudson Valley breeze blowing leaves outside my window like rust-colored rain. After a few moments of quiet I saw an image behind my eyes. It was a circle etched on a black background with a samurai sword centered vertically within it and a bright, red lotus blossom superimposed over the center of the sword. The image reminded me of a *mandala. Mandalas* are the traditional paintings used in monasteries to describe higher worlds of consciousness and which provide adepts challenging tools for focusing their minds. This picture remained fixed in my mind, as clear as if I had been staring at it fully rendered on paper. Soon, it was. An artist was able to reproduce the precise image I had seen in my meditation.

This *mandala* was to become the logo for my company and the visual representation for The Three-Fold Path to Mastery. On the next few pages I have outlined the fundamentals of this philosophy.

THE THREE-FOLD PATH MANDALA

The Three-Fold Path *mandala* comprises a red lotus blossom superimposed on the blade of a samurai sword inside a circle. Together, these elements represent the three pathways to mastery: The Lotus [soft skills], The Sword [professional skills – also called hard skills], and The Circle [continuous improvement]. These components are described in detail on the following pages.

As explained previously, the word *mandala* traditionally describes an intricate painting representing a complex spiritual concept, or a map of an exalted inner world. Buddhist monks will gaze at a *mandala* for hours until they are able to reproduce every pixel of the image in their minds during meditation. Meditating upon the inner painting, they can begin to deepen their understanding of the concept it depicts, or they may even visit within their minds the world it represents, internalizing the light and power it manifests.

The Three-Fold Path *mandala* is a graphical representation of an ideal world that equally balances ethics and etiquette, professional skills and personal growth. Mastery is the art of achieving perfection in work, as a template for polishing one's spirit.

DIAGRAM OF THE THREE-FOLD PATH
TO MASTERY PHILOSOPHY

Here is a diagram including the Keys and Fundamental Principles of The Three-Fold Path to Mastery:

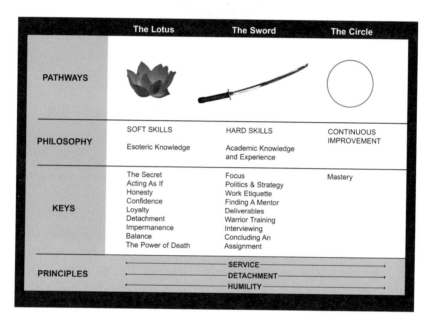

	The Lotus	The Sword	The Circle
PATHWAYS			
PHILOSOPHY	SOFT SKILLS Esoteric Knowledge	HARD SKILLS Academic Knowledge and Experience	CONTINUOUS IMPROVEMENT
KEYS	The Secret Acting As If Honesty Confidence Loyalty Detachment Impermanence Balance The Power of Death	Focus Politics & Strategy Work Etiquette Finding A Mentor Deliverables Warrior Training Interviewing Concluding An Assignment	Mastery
PRINCIPLES	SERVICE DETACHMENT HUMILITY		

Now that you have an overview of the components of The Three-Fold Path to Mastery, we will consider in greater detail The Lotus, Sword and Circle Pathways, as well as the Fundamental Principles of *Service*, *Detachment* and *Humility*.

THE LOTUS

SOFT SKILLS

The lotus is a symbol of enlightenment and purity. It is a flower one finds resting on the surface of the water and though its roots are in the mud, its blossoms always grow towards the light of the sun. The Three-Fold Path uses the red lotus blossom to represent the soft skills, which are to be applied together with professional skills to achieve mastery. Soft skills include the abilities to work with confidence, to act with integrity, to be loyal, to listen to others with compassion and interest, to focus all one's energy on a task while avoiding expectations about the outcome, to recognize the transience of circumstances and states of mind, to remain steady and at peace despite personal challenges, and to embrace every moment of life as a precious gift. The way of attaining a state of fulfillment in work and in life is to grow both personally and spiritually, as well as professionally.

Business schools often neglect entirely to teach their students these less technical, more esoteric skills. Ironically, the lack of these skills is a major complaint of managers in corporations the world over. Embracing the aesthetic of acting ethically and compassionately, we can make our work a source of joy, fulfillment and financial success.

The Samurai Sword

Professional Skills

The samurai sword represents a tool of discrimination, used to cut through the veil of ignorance and illusion and reveal the Truth. The sword is symbolic of the warrior arts, a counterbalance to the creative arts. Warrior arts are those practices that force us to conquer, not others, but ourselves. Warrior arts teach us to face and embrace challenges, using academic knowledge, wisdom and expertise.

In The Three-Fold Path philosophy the sword symbolizes the hard skills, also called professional skills, which one must apply to achieve a goal or succeed in work. These skills include the power to focus exclusively on a single task, to be able to navigate office politics, to behave with refinement and sensitivity, to seek out guidance from experienced individuals in one's field, to present regular evidence of one's efforts, and to cultivate one's mind, body and spirit. It is knowledge, experience and skill in a particular field that enable us to provide the highest service to others. Pursuing continuous education and striving to reach the heights of achievement in our chosen profession lend us the respect and gratitude of others, as well as the joy of leading a productive life.

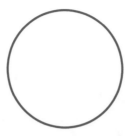

THE CIRCLE

CONTINUOUS IMPROVEMENT

A circle symbolizes perfection. In The Three-Fold Path, we strive to achieve a perfect balance between ethics and etiquette, experience and practical skills, and personal mastery. The circle describes The Three-Fold Path as a continuous process. There is no beginning and no end. There is no time when even a master of The Three-Fold Path will suddenly realize he has no more to achieve, no more to learn, no more room for growth. An individual who believes he has already attained perfection eliminates the possibility of any future evolution. It is the enthusiasm to keep exploring the mysteries of this world and the willingness to learn new ways to explore it that define mastery. Mastery is attained, not by seeking a sense of completion, but by forever embodying the openness and beauty of a beginner. Mastery is not an ending. It is the pursuit of the infinite possibilities and wonder of the future.

FUNDAMENTAL PRINCIPLES
OF THE THREE-FOLD PATH

The Three-Fold Path to Mastery describes how to live and work with greater success and satisfaction by performing any action with the combined attitudes of:

> **Service:** Applying ourselves in service to someone or something else. It is only when we give ourselves over to the implementation of a task in service to a person, organization, goal or ideal that we can at least temporarily forget about our own challenges and thus attain levels of productivity and perfection in our work that a preoccupation with our personal burdens makes impossible.

> **Detachment:** Unhooking ourselves from a fixation with a specific outcome and focusing on the joy and discipline of the process of attaining a goal, rather than the ultimate attainment of it.

> **Humility:** Taking a very humble view of ourselves and our significance in relation to others. Humility also requires the recognition that there may be higher powers responsible for our gifts and achievements, such that we mustn't become overly pleased by our personal accomplishments nor overly despondent over apparent failures.

Applying these Fundamental Principles to every action of our lives, and living and working within the disciplines of the Three Pathways (Sword, Lotus and Circle), we achieve an uncommon life of success and lasting peace. However, you should realize that by attempting to live this way you may find yourself swimming against the stream of mass consciousness.

Living this way requires operating with an entirely different motivation than a large part of the human race embraces. I believe you can break down our entire species into two kinds of people: those who operate from a selfish motivation and those who operate from a self*less* motivation. Only two kinds: selfish or selfless. While most people will make choices and act based on the response to the question, "What's in this for me?", practitioners of The Three-Fold Path make choices and act based on the response to an alternative question, "What can I do for others?" Masters always consider how best they can serve others, better the world, brighten someone else's day, contribute to the greater goal. Selfish people are the ones who will knock you down in order to seize the last bag of rice off an aid truck. And then they likely won't share it.

Selfish people seem to see the universe as providing a limited source of fulfillment and that if you want to succeed, you are in competition with other people for a limited amount of possible attainment. On the other hand, self*less* people see the universe as providing a potentially infinite amount of attainment, available to whomever seeks that. Selfish people see the need to take what they can when they can, and imagine that their taking probably must come *from* someone else, since supply is limited. Selfless people see that there is an unlimited supply of success available, and that they just need to open themselves up to what is already there. Limited supply versus infinite supply. Selfish versus selfless. Here's a simple chart demonstrating the differences between the two approaches.

Selfish	Selfless
Not having	Having
Limited supply	Unlimited supply
Aggressive	Gentle
Success based entirely on individual ability to compete against others and win	Infinite potential for success for everyone based on all possible opportunity in the universe
Arrogant	Humble

This is the way to grasp the power of having a selfless view of the universe. If you give something to others, that creates a reality of *having*. Like dropping a pebble into a lake and watching the ripples widen to encompass the entire surface of the water, giving that which you want to have drops a pebble into the lake of your life, eventually filling it with the truth that you *have* that which you gave. To use very simple examples, if you want to have more money, be more generous. If you need a job, help someone else with his resume or refer him to a contact of yours. Operate from the logical point of view that to give something away you must have it. This creates more energy around you *having* – money or employment or anything else. It creates vibrations, ripples, out into the universe of having.

A selfless approach actually generates a much greater probability of success than a selfish one. The selfish approach is aggressive. You are taking, grabbing, because you believe you won't get another opportunity to have what you want. Here you perpetuate a reality of not having, of needing. The selfless approach is gentle and trusting. You believe that the possibility for your own success is infinite, and so you are open to the opportunities that constantly present themselves.

Selfish people limit their own success. In their very act of taking at the expense of others, they shut off the potentially infinite flow of success that they could have drawn directly from the source.

Finally, a selfish approach is arrogant. It is worship of oneself, rather than faith in a higher power. It is the idea that you have to scratch and steal and claw at the scraps of success because everyone is competing for the few pieces available. The selfless approach is reflected in the third Fundamental Principle of The Three-Fold Path, *Humility*. It respects that one's success is partly due to one's ability to draw directly from the source, a power greater than your own, whatever that may be in your own belief system.

In order to grasp the principles of The Three-Fold Path and the Keys of the Lotus Pathway, it is necessary to understand this fundamental approach to life and work that will help you to discriminate between right and wrong, between ethical choices and unethical ones, between compassionate action and self-serving behavior, between actions that will ultimately bring you fulfillment, success and joy, and those that will not.

After teaching The Three-Fold Path to Mastery over the past few years, I have been privileged to share this philosophy with a wide variety of people, from corporate executives, artists, computer programmers, musicians and others, to teachers and even firefighters. The positive response has been overwhelming and gratifying. One of my most treasured stories of transformation came from a captain in the New York City Fire Department.

On September 11, 2001, Captain Tom O'Brien rushed to the World Trade Center from his station house a few blocks away. Despite years of responding to five alarm fires and disasters of all kinds, nothing had prepared him for the horror he saw that day. Most traumatic was witnessing human beings make the choice to dive out of windows eighty stories above the ground rather than take the chance of waiting inside the towers for a miracle. Bodies crashed onto the pavement. Death was everywhere. Though Captain O'Brien escaped uninjured, the experience scarred him deeply.

I was also in the Wall Street area that morning. As the Twin Towers fell, I was crouched in an office building lobby, debris swirling in the black air outside the glass doors, women and men howling like animals all around me. The stench of the wreckage was fierce. For weeks afterwards I would burst into tears whenever I passed a fire station on my way to work, the entrances filled with the colors of countless bouquets of flowers left by sympathetic New Yorkers. So many heroes lost.

In the winter of 2003 my company reached a milestone of success teaching The Three-Fold Path to Mastery philosophy to individuals and Fortune 500 corporations around the country. It felt like an appropriate time to give back to the world. Immediately I thought of firefighters, those brave men and women that not only sacrificed their lives on 9/11, but who put themselves in harm's way every day so that the rest of us can live in safety. We initiated the Heroes Program in Santa Fe in February 2004, and in March we donated our Three-Fold Path to Mastery seminar along with a copy of my book (an earlier version of *Mastery At Work*) to thirty-three senior members and leaders of the New York Fire Department's Special Operations Command. Shortly after the class I received a letter from one of the attendees that brought me to tears. The letter was from Captain Tom O'Brien, fellow witness to the gruesome events of 9/11. He wrote:

> *Recently, I was chosen to attend a [Three-Fold Path to Mastery] seminar for the FDNY. The class allowed me to "see" so much about myself that day. I sat and read the book that was given at the end of the presentation. It con-*

tinued to reinforce the way I feel I want to live my life
every day. It isn't only about work. It's about life.

Thank you.
Tom O'Brien
Capt FDNY
Squad 18

It was only after I received this letter that I learned more of
Captain O'Brien's story from one of his oldest friends, a volunteer
fireman and salesperson with a national telecom company. His
friend told me about how, after September 11th, "Tommy" was
changed. "He was numb," his friend said, "Before that day he was
always fun and filled with life, but afterwards he was just dead."

For over two and a half years, he told me, Tommy had lost one
of his most defining characteristics: his enthusiasm for living. His
friend ended the call with these words, "You have no idea how
much your class changed him. I got an e-mail from him shortly
after he read your book and he was back to himself, talking about
life and how he wants to live it. He gave your book to me and I
can't wait to read it myself."

This story, and others like it, render completely impotent any
suffering I have experienced in my life, any challenges I have struggled to overcome. It is the opportunity to continue to help others
live meaningful lives that gives meaning to my own. I don't know
how often I succeed, but it is trying that makes life worth living.

Here is a beautiful tale that perfectly illustrates the philosophy
of a person that has chosen to walk The Three-Fold Path to
Mastery:

In 1017 AD in a small village in India a great saint was born.
After many years of seeking Truth, Ramanuja placed himself at the
feet of a spiritual master and begged to be initiated in the most
secret and sacred of all mantras. (A mantra is a powerful word or
phrase that confers blessings and wisdom when chanted repeatedly.) The master consented and whispered the holy words to him,
but with a strict warning never to reveal the mantra to anyone. He
told the young saint, "Whoever hears these sacred sounds will
instantly be liberated from suffering, but the person who reveals
them will be condemned to hell."

Ramanuja bowed in gratitude to the master, and ran to the nearest temple. He gathered a large crowd around him and shouted the secret mantra for all to hear. Seeing the commotion, the master hurried to the temple and realized at once what his initiate had just done. He scolded Ramanuja severely and told him that he would suffer eternal damnation. Ramanuja smiled at the master and replied, "If my damnation can liberate so many people, then my supreme desire is to be damned."

"You have passed the test," the master said, and gave Ramanuja his holy blessing.[i]

Caring for the ultimate success, fulfillment and joy of others, we attain our own, much greater blessing. This is the philosophy of The Three-Fold Path to Mastery and the ultimate story of *Mastery At Work.*

I can only hope that each reader of this book finds as much power and happiness from the words in these pages as I derived from sharing them.

Nicole Grace
August 2005

THE FIRST PATHWAY

THE LOTUS

"Things do not change; we change."
– Henry David Thoreau

KEY #1: THE SECRET

"...We seek to transmute the gross into the subtle and the pure...Very soon our whole being circles around an invisible Sun of splendor, and we are drawn more and more to it, like steel to a magnet."
— *Israel Regardie, The Tree of Life*[ii]

There is a secret to walking The Three-Fold Path to Mastery and to achieving the success, fulfillment and joy that is your birthright. It is a simple secret. And though it is the solution to having everything in life that you want, very few people will actually use this Key to open the door to the treasures that their future holds for them. This secret is *the willingness to change.*

If you do not have the success, fulfillment and joy that you crave, then you must make an adjustment; you must become the kind of person that does have the success, fulfillment and joy you crave. Become. Change.

A Buddhist monk goes up to a hot dog vendor and says, "Make me one with everything." The vendor laughs and says, "That'll be $1.50." The monk hands over $2.00 and waits, but the vendor just smiles and goes back to making his hot dogs. The monk says to him, "Excuse me, what about my change?" The vendor replies, "Change must come from within!"

Most people expect to stay exactly the same, maintain their habitual routines, patterns of behavior and ways of solving problems, and yet at the same time, to miraculously produce new circumstances. An act of grace, of magic, is possible, but it can't be counted on. Perhaps grace will come and you will be blessed, suddenly and unexpectedly, with a completely new life. Perhaps you will guess the winning lottery numbers, the diet pill you bought in the back of a magazine will remove twenty pounds overnight, or you will be offered your dream job working in Hawaii for three times the salary you make now. There's always room for providence. In the meantime, change is up to you. If you want to choose new circumstances, such as a more fulfilling career, a greater sense of purpose, a higher income, a life filled with deeper love, then you have to take action yourself.

1991 winner of the Nobel Peace Prize for leading a non-violent campaign for change against her country's oppressive regime, Burmese heroine Aung San Suu Kyi has said, "We achieve everything by our efforts alone. We decide our own fate by our actions. You have to gain mastery over yourself. . . . It is not a matter of sitting back and accepting." Change is a choice and requires effort. Regardless of our particular government, one oppressive regime we all face is of our own design – our ego.

Nevertheless, the key to change is not just in taking new action. It is the willingness to become someone new as well. If who you are today were able to be as successful, fulfilled and content as you dream of being, then you already would be. So while deciding to do things differently and making subtle changes in your behavior are a good first step, this type of modification is superficial and limited. Ultimately, you have to be willing to change your *nature:* to evolve.

The Three-Fold Path to Mastery provides a yellow brick road for evolution. If you follow the suggestions in this book, if you do the exercises, if you embrace the Fundamental Principles of this path, then you will loosen your hold on an identity and on a method of existing that has not worked for you, and you will enter a state of fluidity that will allow you to recreate yourself. Flexible in nature, you will be free to evolve into the highest, brightest, most successful, most peaceful being you can be.

Truthfully, developing a willingness to change, let alone actually changing, is hard. As we grow older we become exceedingly attached to our identities. Whether we like ourselves all the time or not, we can still be quite proud of ourselves overall. Our creation! Our masterpiece! Our great attainment that we spent 20, 30, 40, 50 years or more sculpting and sanding down! All the suffering you had to pass through in order to become who you are: all the challenges you faced either successfully or not, all the love you have received and expressed, all the self-modification you have achieved through years of social interaction and politicking. It's hard to give that up.

The willingness to change requires a recognition that whatever you have achieved and whomever you have become is not enough. Otherwise, you would be utterly content. You can acquire magnificent objects, homes, cars and jewelry. You can work in a fantastic cosmopolitan city or travel to holy lands on retreat. But wherever you go, there you are. In the end you will never find what you are looking for by hunting for it someplace else. The only lasting source of peace and well-being is found in your own self.

Continuous work on your masterpiece is required in order to continue to reach for higher goals. Being so set in your ways that you can no longer take positive steps forward is attachment in the extreme. It's relatively easy to give up more tangible things, such as giving up free time in order to work longer hours, or giving up savings in order to buy more impressive evidence of your success. What is more difficult to do is to give up your image of yourself; for example, as someone who doesn't have success and can't ever have it. Don't worry about how to change. The 18 Keys will show you. For now, embrace the willingness to change and the change will come.

The most famous Buddhist mantra is "Om mani padme hum." It is pronounced "ohm-mahnee-pahdmay-hoom." Translated from the Sanskrit it means, literally, "The jewel is in the lotus." Buddhists believe that the words of this mantra carry a vibration that, when either spoken out loud or repeated inside the mind, is so powerful it can heal the world of suffering. In plain words, the mantra means that enlightenment is in all things. Ecstatic bliss, light and perfection are present inside the lotus, inside you. You simply need to uncover the jewel. Evolution is not so much an acquiring of something missing as it is a removal of the obstacles that prevent you from seeing and benefiting from what is already present inside you. Repeating these words is like repeating an affirmation of your potential to have the greatest gifts imaginable. You don't need to repeat this mantra, though it can't hurt...but you may want to internalize its message and repeat that to yourself as a powerful motivator for achieving your goals.

Your potential to be joyful and truly content in your life is a given. The Three-Fold Path to Mastery will help you to reveal this potential.

The willingness to change, the secret, the Key to revealing your treasures, is the willingness to scrub away the old routines, the rusty patterns of thought and the modes of operating that have obscured your own light from shining.

As you walk through the 18 Keys of The Three-Fold Path to Mastery, try to release your resistance to embracing these core principles. The greatest resistance will manifest in the belief that you have already mastered them. Don't make this mistake. This is a trap that will prevent all growth. As we will discover in the Circle Pathway, the very definition of mastery is a state in which you feel there is always room for further evolution.

You may find that you have achieved an integration in your own life of many of these principles and tools. Nevertheless, consider each Key an opportunity to explore your understanding of these attributes in greater depth.

In any discussion referring to mastery, it is helpful to consider the third Fundamental Principle of the philosophy: *Humility*. Though you may feel validated by some of the Keys of the Lotus Pathway or Sword Pathway, it is humility that you must cling to like an old lady guarding her purse. You can suffer the temporary loss of qualities like Confidence or Balance or Focus. But in the absence of humility, all evolution ceases. In other words, if you believe you have already reached the summit, you won't keep climbing. Keep humility foremost in your mind as you consider each Key and the integration of its wisdom in your life.

Finally, remember that your ultimate evolution is up to you. Don't be satisfied by superficial representations of success, fulfillment and joy. Don't give up your striving to be better, wiser, nobler, kinder just because you have received validation from the world of some level of attainment. Just as the Circle implies, mastery is about continuous improvement, never ceasing the journey.

There's a hilarious scene in the movie "Ace Ventura II: When Nature Calls" starring Jim Carrey. In the beginning of the movie, a gentleman interested in recruiting Ace Ventura for a mission treks to a monastery in the mountains where Ace has been on retreat. He asks for Ace by name, but the head monk replies, "No man here carries with him a label." So the man explains, "He bends over and speaks from his rear." (If you have not seen the original "Ace Ventura: Pet Detective" you won't get the reference, though I recommend watching both of these wonderfully silly movies.) Hearing this, the monk recognizes Ace at once and, anxious to get rid of this crazy resident, he swiftly takes the gentleman to Ace's room. Unfortunately, Ace does not want to leave the monastery. "I have yet to attain omnipresent super-galactic oneness!" he protests. "No, wait. There it is," the monk says, pointing to the space around Ace's head, "You've just attained it. You are one! I can see it in your eyes. You are more one than anyone!" Ace insists, "But what about my medallion of spiritual accomplishment?" The monk rips his own medallion off his neck and cries, "Take mine!" [iii]

Don't be satisfied with a medallion. Let the willingness, or better yet the enthusiasm, for personal change motivate your choices in every area of your life. Regardless of how your world reflects back to you your achievements – whether you are glorified or ignored – keep striving. The heart of the lotus must be polished constantly to keep the jewel sparkling.

In the world of business change occurs constantly, an ebb and flow over which we as individuals engaged in business have no control. Change in our environment can be alarming, even when positive. The Holmes-Rahe Social Readjustment Scale[iv] ranks marriage and "outstanding personal achievement" in the top twenty-five most stressful experiences involving change. Even the experiences most people would consider highlights of their lives can induce health-threatening levels of stress. How, then, can we survive the inevitable flux of circumstances we face at work? Companies are constantly merging, upsizing, downsizing, relocating, installing new software and eliminating the applications we know how to use. Given the Social Readjustment Scale's report, even getting promoted can cause anxiety and pain.

What we can do is continue to work on our own evolution. Becoming used to change inwardly, we will find that this fluidity of consciousness overlaps into a greater acceptance of change outside ourselves. The ability to accept and handle change will also make us much more adept at providing service to others. Sometimes acting in a way that is outside our habitual nature can provide the best solution for a person, organization or ideal we are working for.

For example, when a friend or colleague is confiding in you, sometimes it is appropriate to listen quietly. Other times, it is important to share something you've experienced in order to help him understand his own situation. Either way, you would do anything in order to help your friend; even if that means modifying your normal behavior in order to offer yourself in service. A friend's crisis can cause us to suppress what we may want or want to do at a particular moment, and to instead become whatever kind of person he needs at that time.

Dedicated service to others, to a company, organization, goal or ideal, is no different. As we strive for perfection, seeking each day to remove layers of tarnish from our jewel, we embrace all manner of change as the vehicle for realizing our goals. Helping others to attain their goals will soon reveal itself to be the most powerful vehicle for attaining our own, and for effecting a more dramatic transformation in our consciousness than we could ever achieve seeking success only for ourselves.

As you evolve, remember how frightening you once found this secret of happiness. Your colleagues, friends and family may find your evolution frightening at first. George Bernard Shaw said, "The only man I know who behaves sensibly is my tailor; he takes my measurements anew each time he sees me. The rest go on with their old measurements and expect me to fit them." Keep altering the measurements of your growth to accommodate your progress. Eventually, you will inspire others to seek their own evolution through the example of your immeasurably improved life.

CHAPTER SUMMARY

THE SECRET

- The secret to achieving success, fulfillment and joy is the willingness to change.
- This willingness will make you fluid enough to achieve great personal evolution.
- Embracing personal change will prepare you for accepting and balancing change in your work life.
- Change is a continuous process. Mastery is realizing you will never be done.
- Remember as you change, that others around you might be frightened by this. Show them by example the joy of a commitment to evolving.

CHAPTER EXERCISES

THE SECRET

1. *Experimenting with Change*

Here's a simple exercise you can do to determine how you respond to change. Chances are that you will enjoy the results of this test. The hard part is getting yourself to do things like this more often.

a) Pick a room in your house or apartment whose appearance has remained the same for a long time. It should be a room or area that you pass through every day.

b) Before you leave for work one morning or right before you go to sleep, change one significant aspect of this room. Replace a picture on the wall with a new one or rearrange one or more pieces of furniture.

c) When you first notice the change, either when you return home from work or when you wake up the next morning, how do you feel? Do you notice anything different over the next two days, even when you are not home?

Rearranging even one piece of furniture can make a surprising difference in your perception of your surroundings. A great time to do this exercise is right before you leave on a trip, so that the change is more noticeable upon your return. It is also an effective way of welcoming yourself home after you have had a transformational experience. (When you have been on vacation or you have done something different from your usual routine, you will inevitably experience some transformation, however insignificant.) It can actually feel more uncomfortable to return home to the same old house, the same old patterns, than to come home to a place that feels fresh and different. The changed environment can more easily accommodate your transformed self.

2. *Shifting Routines*

This is another deceptively simple exercise that will make you feel surprisingly refreshed and open to new challenges.

a) For one day (how about tomorrow?), totally shift every routine and pattern you normally follow.

b) For example:

   i) Change the order in which you normally go through your morning ritual; so if you normally shower before you grab breakfast, eat first and then shower. Brush your teeth with your other hand. Put on music if you normally have a quiet morning. And so on.

   ii) Take a different route to work; take a different mode of transportation. (You may have figured out the fastest way to get to the office, but you may discover, for example, a hidden-away, mouth-watering pastry shop along a route you have never tried.)

   iii) Eat or buy your lunch somewhere you have never gone before.

   iv) After you get home (having taken a different route than usual) do something out of character with your downtime, however brief that may be. If you normally watch a video, go for a walk. If you normally read, sing along with the radio for ten minutes first.

c) Now that you have the idea, give this a try. Do everything differently for one day and see how you feel the next day and the day after that. Did you discover anything unexpected? Don't make this a one-time exercise. Try it once a month and see if you notice any more significant changes after six months.

KEY #2: ACTING AS IF

"Truth, truth, truth alone will have the glory. The reality, the real character, the sterling character alone will have the glory and will have success."
                                               – Swami Rama Tirtha[v]

The greatest obstacle most people have in realizing their dreams is not financial or practical, but simply one of belief. As human beings, we are always dreaming about being better versions of ourselves. Occasionally we decide to take steps towards actually realizing those dreams. However, the most significant step we can take is quiet and internal. To believe. To believe that becoming better, wealthier, kinder, more intelligent and nobler is possible. But how?

Our world's most remarkable heroes, celebrities and people of achievement have one thing in common: they each reached a point where they believed their own success was possible. I have been told that Oprah Winfrey is so famous and so successful that she has become a cliché. So be it. Cliché or not, I would like us to consider the story of this extraordinary self-made woman, one of the highest paid entertainers in history and the first African American woman on the Forbes list of American billionaires. Oprah helped create a nationally syndicated talk show, a popular lifestyle magazine and a cable network, all of which have been an inspiration to countless individuals. Her generosity is legendary: she purchases expensive gifts for staff members, donates homes to underprivileged families through her Angel Network and gives away millions of dollars to charity every year. Having reached the heights of achievement, Oprah now uses her power to help others.

It's important to look at how someone this accomplished got

that way, to understand how it was done. Her success was not a foregone conclusion. Born to a poor family in rural Mississippi and a troublemaker until her early teens, she did not have a promising early life. She was faced with many agonizing choices during her rise to stardom, and the steps she took were only made possible each time by her belief that she could succeed in a new role, in a new type of career. In 1991 she told an interviewer, "In the fourth grade was when I first, I think, began to believe in myself. For the first time believed I could do almost anything."

Even for Oprah, though, belief continued to be a struggle. After achieving modest success on television, she was presented with an opportunity to have her own show. She commented, "When my lawyer first came to me and said, 'You can own your own show,' it literally took the ceiling off my brain because I had never even thought that high before. I never even thought that was possible." *vi*

If thinking "high" continued to be a challenge for someone as accomplished as Oprah Winfrey, how then can ordinary people, who have yet to realize their potential, get to the point of believing in the possibility of their own success? Very simply. By *Acting As If*. Believing in herself, Oprah raised herself from poverty to wealth, from obscurity to global icon.

In this Key we'll explore how the art of envisioning we have characteristics and skills such as confidence, leadership, poise, expertise and refinement can be used in order to develop and genuinely possess these traits in the future. Ultimately, on The Three-Fold Path we don't fake it, we learn it. First we work on believing we can achieve greatness, and then we get to work doing whatever it takes to actually be great.

Acting As If means going through all the motions of being someone or something, even though you don't yet believe you actually are that person or thing. *Acting As If* can bring us closer to our goals, just by allowing us to envision ourselves as having already attained them. It is not an act of dishonesty, but rather an act of power. *Acting As If* is a way of honoring your own unrealized potential, of removing the psychological obstacles to your success that have been weighing you down, setting you free to attain unlimited wealth, fulfillment, power, joy and peace.

Part of the difficulty in achieving personal change is in convincing oneself that it is possible. We hold a specific type of person in high regard, put them on a pedestal. From our vantage point, we can't imagine ever being like that person.

When I was training for my black belt in karate, I realized that I had so deified people who had black belts, that I couldn't imagine ever having that rank myself. A few months prior to my final test I actually stopped going to class for a while because I was so terrified of attaining my goal. It may sound illogical, but it was the possibility of *success* that was preventing me from doing what was necessary to attain it, rather than the possibility of failure. Since then, I have encountered numerous other people who confided that they were more afraid of success than of failure. Regardless of whether your fear is of failure or success, the important point to note is that we tend to put obstacles in our own path to prevent ourselves from rising to new levels, professionally and personally. The way I finally got myself to start attending karate classes again was by imagining myself with a black belt already tied around my waist, instead of the brown belt I had been wearing for several years. I had to negotiate with my psyche, with my perception of what I could achieve, in order to allow myself to transform beyond my comfortable levels of success. Every night before I went to sleep, I would imagine bowing to my teacher after promotion and watching him tie a new black belt around my white canvas uniform.

It happens that the technique I used to create belief in my ability to promote to black belt is similar to one called "imagery," used by top sports psychologists like Dr. Peter Jensen to help Olympic athletes bring their skills to new heights and, of course, to win medals. In an article for the *Atlantis Newsletter,* Jensen describes imagery in action: "Figure skater Elizabeth Manley (silver medalist at the Calgary Oympics) would walk out beside the rink boards during the warm-up of the group skating prior to her. She felt the crowd around her, taking in the whole environment from a perspective as close as possible to the real thing – one foot away from the ice. She also used imagery once she had completed her on-ice warm-up. She would walk through her entire program when she was two skaters away from performing. While waiting out the final five minutes before her performance, she would focus her imagery and walk through the first section of her program only. When Elizabeth stepped onto the ice to perform, her mind and body were at ease, for to them, they had already been there and had completed a perfect performance." *vii*

In business we can utilize the technique of imagery to transform into a more educated, more experienced, better dressed and better paid version of ourselves. We can take the principle of imagery and apply it to actions, not just by envisioning ourselves in a dream state where we are wiser and better dressed, but by actually dressing better and actually advancing our professional skills. In this way we can force ourselves into becoming the kind of person we previously thought we could never be or even be like.

Though we may have days where we feel like cowering behind a plant in our boss' office, we must *Act As If* we are the perfect leader, hold our head high, and speak with authority and compassion. By pretending we are confident, by acting with understanding, we will eventually become confident, become understanding.

Slowly, as we overcome our own self-doubt, through self-affirmation, we will be able to project that confidence from within.

There are two primary methods for putting *Acting As If* into practice. These are pursuing *Continuous Education* and *Projecting the Image.*

Continuous Education

Acting As If does not mean pretending to have skills you don't have. This is an important point. It means being capable of envisioning yourself with those skills, and then *working hard to acquire them* once the obstacle of belief has been conquered. The first step towards becoming more successful is *believing* you can learn to program a computer, speak a foreign language, or give a presentation. The next very important step is doing whatever it takes to reach those goals.

Both experience in and academic knowledge of one's field are the practical elements of being successful. The ultimate goal of mastery requires transcending ordinary success. This requires attaining significant expertise in a particular area, as well as being exposed to new and even unrelated subjects that complement your existing knowledge, or that just make you well-rounded and happy.

Becoming an expert in any area, of course, takes time. You can read a hundred books about your industry, but without practical experience, you will be lacking an essential foundation upon which your work must be based. Nevertheless, there is still a way to distinguish yourself in the short term: through an evolving awareness of your field. By continuously expanding your consciousness, learning new things constantly, you will find yourself exceeding your colleagues' and employer's expectations for your abilities, and soon even your own.

Here are some ideas for expanding your education:

1) Have an educational goal. This can be annual. For example, to achieve a working understanding of a particular technology within 12 months. Or, it can be longer term: to obtain a PhD in a particular subject within the next 6 years. Here are some examples of educational goals:

   a) Earn a certificate, degree or advanced degree in your professional field

   b) Learn a new technology

   c) Explore a new, related field to complement your current work

   d) Learn something completely unrelated to work, but which makes you happy

   e) Learn to write

      The power of good, strong writing skills is of tremendous professional benefit. You would be surprised how many people have appalling grammar and spelling, and flaunt that regularly. Daily business often requires documenting your work, writing reports, sending letters and e-mail. Strong writing has power and people can feel it. If you know writing or grammar is a weakness of yours, endeavor to change that now.

2) Take classes on the side.

a) Try web-based learning

b) Take off a few weeks, or a month, from work to join an accelerated learning program or certificate training class

c) Take classes at night or on weekends – sacrifice a year or two with long days for a lifetime of living with more knowledge and bigger paychecks

Continuing your education throughout your life keeps your mind fresh, engaged and open to new possibilities. You can never know too much. (Adapting the famous Beverly Hills philosophy: *You can never be too rich, too thin, or too educated.*) By always seeking new opportunities to learn, you will maintain a mental agility, an attitude of curiosity, and a unique perspective on problem solving that we often lose as we grow older.

If you are beginning a new work assignment and you know that you are weak in a particular skill that you may need on the job, learn it. Even if your employer knows you are not strong in that area and wanted you to work for him anyway – learn the skill. For example, if your job is to manage a team of software developers, you may not need to know how to program computers yourself, but it is still a good idea to be familiar with the product they are using.

Buy a book on the subject in which you are weak. Buy magazines with relevant, recent articles on the product or knowledge area you don't know. Remember Captain James T. Kirk of the starship Enterprise (from the classic TV show "Star Trek")? Remember how the crew trusted him and obeyed his every command? Captain Kirk knew every section, nut, bolt and screw on that ship and how to fix it. Leaders are experts. Fill in the gaps in your repertoire of professional skills and you will distinguish yourself from the average person who just shows up for work, fulfilling his duties with minimum effort, using his existing – however lacking – skill set. Average people don't grow or change that often. Average people seek comfort. Learning can be demanding. It will expand your horizons and challenge your views. It will also make your mind flexible and open to new ways of seeing problems, and help you to recognize innovative solutions. People who continually challenge themselves and who approach their work with verve always get noticed, and often get rewarded with opportunities for career advancement as well as financial incentives. Knowledge, and the ability to apply it practically, will make you a leader. It will give you power. It will change you.

Projecting the Image

Attire

In the movie "Working Girl," an administrative assistant named Tess McGill (played by Melanie Griffith) is able to pass herself off as a senior executive by putting on her boss' expensive clothes, changing her hairstyle and refining her manners. Tess manages to effect this significant transformation almost overnight. After two weeks of pretending to be her boss, she actually becomes capable of doing that job. Tess was already highly intelligent, but making a dramatic career jump from an administrative assistant to an executive seemed unrealistic at first. Her boss and her colleagues consistently reinforced in her the idea that she could never hope to succeed at such a high level. However, by *Acting As If* she were in charge, by changing her appearance to that of an executive, Tess convinced the executives of another company, and she convinced herself, that she was in charge and that she was an executive. Allowing herself to step into the role of someone she wanted to be like, she was able to overcome her self-doubt and the limited view others maintained of her.

Effecting a more refined appearance is not just a Halloween-like game of dress-up. It can create a powerful psychological cue to others that you possess the qualities associated with a person who dresses in a particular way.

Have you ever encountered someone in business who was so impeccably dressed that the person's presence actually intimidated you? Many top salespeople have figured out how to dress in a way that intimidates people. This makes us see them as authority figures and makes us eager to take their advice, or buy the product they are selling. Celebrities have an intimidating effect on us as well. Often, it is not the fact that a celebrity is famous that makes us react to them with awe, but rather the person's ability to present themselves with such flawlessness. Perfection is a bit scary. Seeing outer perfection in others makes us assume they are perfect inside, as well. It may not be true, but we react to outer perfection with respect regardless. (Practicing The Three-Fold Path to Mastery, we work on both inner and outer perfection.) We treat people who have a refined appearance like superheroes, masters, accomplished human beings who must have figured out something we have not.

Movie star Rita Hayworth was aware of the power of appearance. Born Rita Cansino, she changed her name, dyed her hair red and dressed herself like a goddess, perpetuating the studio-created image of her as an untouchable, flawless beauty. In reality she was a talented, beautiful actress, but still an earthbound human being. Referring to the role that made her a star, she famously said, "Men go to bed with Gilda and wake up with me." She understood that men would fall in love with the legend, but wake up with the reality. Nevertheless, she maintained her image in public as part of her career. That helped her to get into character when on set, and it transformed her from a good actress into a Hollywood legend. She played the role of "star" on and off the set, and thus became one.

A perfectly cultivated appearance is an act of magic. A deliberately engineered outfit is alchemy. It has the power to transform a brilliant administrative assistant into an executive in a few weeks. It can reveal to a roomful of people that you are capable, intelligent and worthy. Hopefully, you will even convince yourself.

Dressing impeccably requires energy. Over time, through continuing our education, gaining experience, living a healthy life, and making ethical choices we can increase our level of energy. As we evolve, our appearance will evolve with us. Nevertheless, a little bit of magic can be applied before we have attained greatness, to further the process along.

A professional, meticulous and polished appearance is an outward expression of existing inner, personal power. Power can be gained by polishing from the outside in: by first *Acting As If,* then *becoming.*

The type of appearance you should cultivate is particular to your profession. A management consultant might wear an immaculately tailored suit, while a golf pro might wear khaki shorts and a polo shirt. Nevertheless, people from all professions seek to project authority, experience, wisdom and success.

Hone your image over time. You may be surprised how difficult it is at first to put yourself together at a level above your current mode of dressing.

Certain clothes have more power than others. The exclusivity of a label can indicate a higher level of polish in the cut and fabric that are used. It is always advisable to have one good, expensive suit or relevant professional outfit. If you have to wear the same outfit frequently until you can afford others, that is preferable to owning many different ones of lower quality. Build your wardrobe over time.

Your clothes should always look freshly pressed. If you live in a warm climate, look for fabrics that don't easily wrinkle. If you think this doesn't matter, stand outside at lunch hour and watch people walk out of their office buildings. Observe the difference between those wearing unwrinkled clothes and those wearing wrinkled ones. Wrinkled outfits unfortunately give an impression of someone who is a bit sloppy, harried, beset by life. Think of the stereotypical college professor, or Columbo.

Someone in an immaculate, unwrinkled suit looks impressive. If that suit is nicely cut and, preferably, dark, the person appears professional, capable. A person who dresses sharply – with a well-matched suit and tie, or suit and scarf, with a good briefcase and shined shoes – seems to pay attention to every detail. This person appears to be strong and in control.

Working for companies who have adopted a business casual dress code can make dressing impeccably more complicated. How can it be done in a workplace where everyone is wearing khakis and polo shirts, for example?

Observe people entering and leaving the office. Consider how people dress in different departments, particularly your own department and the sales department, and make sure to get a peek at what the company executives are wearing. Use executives as a guide for the high end of appropriate dress code when possible. If everyone wears polo shirts, buy particularly nice polo shirts, wear them tucked in and iron your pants. Wear good shoes. If you are a woman, wear some makeup, even in a casual office.

Smell

Make sure not to use lotions, hair gels, or any other personal cosmetics that have a strong odor. Never wear perfume or cologne to the office. What is the purpose of these items? To give off a particularly noticeable odor, to smell better than others, to evoke a mood or draw attention. All of these are reasons why smells don't belong in the office. What matters in the office is being neat and clean, productive, unobtrusive and technically proficient.

A colleague used to regale me with hilarious stories about a Global Director (GB) in the entertainment conglomerate where she worked. This gentleman always wore expensive, but extremely strong, cologne. She would joke that people could smell him entering the lobby from the 23rd floor. When women attended meetings with the GB, they would roll their eyes at each other in the hallway and whisper, "Does he *actually* think that stuff is a turn-on or something? My eyes are watering from the smell!" The GB's management skills and intelligence began to take second place after his cologne in everyone's mind. It became a source of ridicule and distraction from whatever his real talents may have been.

When someone walks by you and he (or she) smells of cologne or perfume, you immediately think of him as a person with whatever lifestyle that scent reminds you of, or you think of someone you know who smells like that, or some memory is dislodged that is associated with this smell. If you are interested in excelling professionally, you probably don't want to be in the business of evoking such intimate emotions from your business colleagues. As a practitioner of the art of service, your goal is to accomplish as much as you can, to help others accomplish as much as they can, and to vastly contribute to the attainment of your employer's goals. All the attention you attract in the workplace should be focused on your abilities, not your sexuality.

Women & Appearance

While women's opportunities in the workplace are well on the road to equality with men, there is still disparity in pay and, unfortunately, respect. A major Wall Street investment bank was found guilty of discriminatory practices as recently as July 2004 and was required to pay millions of dollars in reparation to the women in the class action suit. There are still too many examples of these injustices, though corporations are taking steps to correct generations of socialization that women are not equal to men that lie at the root of this issue. One of the areas where women can subtly gain more respect is in the way they present themselves physically.

Dress

Attire is an unusually powerful tool women can use in order to keep the focus, ironically, away from their appearance. By dressing strategically, women can eliminate one more reason for not being appreciated for their intelligence and professional contributions to an organization's goals. Women shouldn't dress just like men do, but must be exceedingly careful not to swing too far in the other direction either, dressing too provocatively. Polished trouser suits are excellent for projecting an image that is both professional and stylish. It's a good idea to tie your hair back if it is long, and keep your nails polished in a nude or sheer color. Once you have achieved a solid reputation and success in your field, some creativity with style is allowed. Nevertheless, caution and extremely good taste should always be applied.

Strive to keep the focus on what you do and not on what you look like.

Suits or business casual outfits that are well-made and simple, in dark colors, are ideal. Stripes, bright colors, out-of-the-ordinary designs, high above the knee skirts, stiletto heels, and big earrings are not ideal. Call attention to your expertise and brilliance, not to your gender.

Makeup

You might assume, from the suggestions above, that it would be ideal for a woman not to wear makeup. On the contrary, makeup is an excellent professional tool for creating an image – a "persona" – to be while you are in the office. Makeup, like suits, should be understated. However, always wear lipstick. Volunteer organizations and college campuses are two of the few acceptable places to avoid lipstick. In a business office, you are not necessarily aiming for that "natural look." You are aiming to project an image.

Makeup is a mask. Wearing makeup doesn't mean you are trading on your looks to get ahead. Makeup allows you to act differently from the way you might otherwise, unadorned and unchanged. Wearing makeup and a suit can feel like a costume, allowing you to be an actor in a drama where you are a star, an executive, a CEO. Wearing a costume, you may be better able to stretch your boundaries of confidence and voice your opinions, be a leader. Our society for the most part continues to further the equality of women. Nevertheless, some conditioning from childhood may linger: conditioning from education, society and media images that depicts women as weaker, quiet, or not bright in math, science and computer technology. If you have trouble believing in yourself as an executive, *Acting As If* you are one can help convince you otherwise.

Finally, consider where most women never wear makeup: at home alone, while sleeping, in the company of close friends. Personally, I find a lack of makeup to be quite intimate. Walking around without any lipstick at all makes me feel very personal, almost vulnerable. I'll wear a bit of makeup at the office simply to distinguish that environment psychologically from my private moments at home.

The objective in utilizing our appearance as a business tool is to create a state of belief in others, as well as in ourselves, of our potential for greatness.

The Guest

When you dress well and look good, people like to have you around. If you are a bit rough around the edges, your hair is unkempt, or you're not clean-shaven, you're just like everybody else. It takes time to dress well, it takes a certain finesse. The time and attention you spend are worthwhile. As someone interested in rising to the top of your profession, your image matters. People should be impressed by you. You should take care in presenting yourself well.

Your appearance is like your resume. You hone it gradually.

Take pleasure in composing yourself more precisely and stylishly all the time. Your presentation is, as we said in the beginning of this section, an outward expression of your inner polish. You will find that you will naturally start looking better as you become more of an inner master.

You might say that as individuals acting with an attitude of service towards organizations, goals or ideals, practitioners of The Three-Fold Path to Mastery are like guests in other people's lives. You have been invited into someone's workplace, perhaps for a limited time, to accomplish a particular task. As a guest, act like one. Dress well and act politely. You will make a good first impression, you will be appreciated, and you will be invited back.

CHAPTER SUMMARY

ACTING AS IF

- *Acting As If* can bring you closer to your goals, by allowing you to envision yourself as having already attained them
- Always have an educational goal
  - Take classes, keep learning
- Polish your image
  - Have at least one good suit
  - Be extremely well-groomed
  - Smell neutral (no perfume, cologne, or heavily scented lotion)
- Act like a guest
  - Be exceptionally polite, and you'll be invited back

CHAPTER EXERCISES

ACTING AS IF

1. *Continuing Education*

Starting a new course of education can feel like a big step. Becoming a student again, if you have been out of school for more than a few years, may seem daunting. If you don't feel ready to make a decision about semester-long courses, start with a small step. Once you get back into the habit of learning and studying, you may feel more comfortable – and even more excited – about signing up for a more significant course of continuing education.

a) Sign Up For Classes
   Sign up for a day-long seminar or one hour instructional class. You don't even need to take a class that is relevant to your profession. Learning anything new will get the little gray cells firing and flexible. Here are a few offbeat suggestions to choose from or to use for inspiration in selecting your own:
   - Pottery class
   - Foreign language – start at the beginning, or just take a conversation class
   - Painting
   - Musical instrument – piano and guitar are good ones to start with
   - History
   - Cooking
   - Golf
   - Typing
   - HTML or another web programming language
   - Public speaking

b) Self-Educate

If you don't have time to take one of the classes suggested above, buy a book on a subject that fascinates you, or one that will further your career, and set aside time for reading it. Do all the exercises in the back of the book, or buy a workbook on the subject and follow the course of study on your own schedule. Dedicate one or two evenings per week to learning this new subject.

c) Visit Professional Organizations

Research professional organizations either in your current field or in the field you want to work in someday. Log onto their websites and find out about local chapter meetings in your area. Most organizations have open nights when they allow non-members to attend their meetings. You'll get a chance to see what kind of people are involved in your field of interest, you'll be able to hear interesting talks from people who are accomplished in the profession, and you'll also have the opportunity to network with other people doing what you love. Sign up for a new meeting this week! Perhaps one day, you may even be the person speaking when other new attendees show up...

2. *Image*

A polished wardrobe is built very deliberately, over time. While you may feel frustrated not to be able to fling open your closet tomorrow and find a rack full of Armani suits, there are small changes you can make that will shift your perspective immediately about the image you are presenting to the world. Here are some simple changes you can make right away, without taking out a second mortgage:

a) Shop

Women: buy the most expensive, chic scarf you can afford. Men: go for an exquisite designer tie. Or, depending on your profession, select another, more appropriate accessory that you can afford to buy, and that you can wear to work right away. Take your time selecting the right item. Go to stores you might normally feel are out of reach – go to Madison Avenue in New York, Rodeo Drive in Beverly Hills, or any of the equivalent high-end shopping areas in your city. Dress nicely when you go on this important mission. Believe that you deserve to wear clothes from these stores. Resist the urge to make this purchase at an outlet or discount department store. Treat yourself to the entire experience of shopping at a different income level. Then, whenever you wear this item, even though it is just a small accessory, you will remember the whole experience that went along with acquiring it. You will carry with you the inner smile of having been king or queen for a day. This will give your item a unique power. One day soon you will be buying your whole outfit this way.

b) Change For Success

Pick a day and dress as if you are at least one level higher up than you currently are. For example, if you are an administrative assistant, dress as if you are an assistant manager. If you are an executive, dress as if you are the CEO of your own company. You may need to come up with a quick answer to questions about your new look. You will be surprised how a slightly modified appearance affects the people you work with! Some of your colleagues may even get angry about it. As you will see, not everyone welcomes change – even if it is positive. Some people might even assume you are heading to an interview after work. To allay fears, prepare a response. If you are too shy to transform your appearance on a workday, it's acceptable to try out your improved attire on a weekend. Take time to chase all the details of your outfit. Stockings and socks count, too! Polish your shoes, do your hair, everything. Then, plan an hour or two of errands. Go to a coffee shop you don't normally frequent and observe how the counterperson treats your more accomplished-looking self. Do errands at shops where you will be recognized, as well. See if you feel different when interacting with people in this new attire.

c) Finally, incorporate some of your new look in your dress every day. You may find that you actually start to see yourself as capable of doing the job of your superiors. Remember, belief is the first and most significant step towards progress.

KEY #3: HONESTY

"Honesty is the first chapter of the book of wisdom."
— Thomas Jefferson

Prominent football coach George O'Leary was hired by Notre Dame in 2001, after helping Georgia Tech earn Bowl invitations five years in a row. The university praised their new coach for his talent, as well as for his impressive background, including a master's degree in education from New York University and three years of playing winning college football for New Hampshire. The problem was that O'Leary had never graduated from NYU and New Hampshire said that he had never even played a single game, let alone scored, on their football team. Five days after they hired him, Notre Dame asked O'Leary for his resignation. Notre Dame athletic director Kevin White issued the following statement to the press: "I understand that these inaccuracies represent a very human failing; nonetheless, they constitute a breach of trust that makes it impossible for us to go forward with our relationship."[viii]

While George O'Leary's dishonesty about his background may have gotten him a few rungs higher on the ladder of success more quickly than he might have climbed otherwise, his unethical behavior cost him dearly later on. His reputation will be tarnished by his false self-promotion forever. Additionally, as a university coach, his dishonesty also harmed others. Is lying to get ahead really the message he would have wanted to send to the college students who looked up to him as an authority figure and mentor?

Most people would define honesty as the quality of speaking or alluding to the truth. But what is the truth? Mystics and saints speak of Truth with a capital "T," as the essence of everything there is: all of consciousness, light, the universe, eternity, God. Thus, we could understand honesty as the quality of speaking about, alluding to or *being aligned with* eternity. Speaking and acting honestly has power, because it allows us to draw directly from the source of all light and consciousness. Speaking and acting dishonestly puts us in conflict with eternity, in opposition to power. Studies have shown that lying causes involuntary, physical responses in the body, such as changes in blood pressure and breathing. These physiological changes, however subtle, can be measured, which is essentially how lie detectors function. Though some people have figured out how to fool the machine, the concept of the tests proves that there is a part of our consciousness that is aware of, and made uncomfortable by, the act of lying. On some level we are aware of the conflict and danger of misaligning ourselves with eternity. The danger is in weakening our link with the source of our power, of all power.

Mark Twain famously said, "If you tell the truth, you don't have to remember anything." Dishonesty breeds an industry of compensating activity: you need to remember the story you told, you need to make up details to support your story, you need to continue to lie and evade in order to prevent others from finding out about your original deceit.

If we apply all our energy towards being successful, honestly and ethically, then we are more likely to become successful and stay successful, than if we squander our energy needlessly covering up half-truths and schemes to get ahead.

There are two essential ways of living and working in alignment with Truth, and for demonstrating honesty to your employers: being honest and sounding honest.

Be Honest

As we learned from the cautionary tale of George O'Leary, lying about your skills rarely pays off in the end. In fact, I have found that employers appreciate when you are completely up front with them about what you can and cannot do so substantially that they will often favor you as a candidate above others who they sense may not be telling the whole truth about their abilities, but who on the surface may seem more accomplished.

It may be tempting, when put on the spot, to say you are capable of doing things that in reality you don't know how to do. Imagine you are being interviewed for a fantastic new job or opportunity, and you are asked whether you have a particular skill or technical expertise. If it seems the only thing standing between you and getting this job or assignment is an insignificant little technical skill, which you kind of sort of saw someone else doing and could probably do...Stop right there. Don't say you can do it. You have arrived at one of life's critical moments: the opportunity to choose whether to take the high road, or a very big chance with your future.

You may set out on a new course today, choosing to act honestly from this point forward. What about small transgressions you may have committed in the past? You will probably find that others are more understanding of your past misconduct when you reveal the truth yourself, as opposed to something you tried to conceal being revealed inadvertently. My father is an attorney and over the years he has seen countless examples of defendants who received much lighter sentences than they might have, because they admitted their mistakes to the judge right away and sincerely expressed remorse for their actions.

People seem to feel that whoever misled them also believed they were too stupid to figure out the truth for themselves. If your lie is ever discovered, the lasting resentment of the person you lied to will far exceed any negative emotions they will feel if you just have the courage to come clean about past misjudgments or mistakes now. Saying you can do things you cannot implies that you either believe you can fool your employer and colleagues, or that you are lazy and you don't want to bother to do what is necessary to get a job on real merit. Start today on a course of honest speech and action.

Despite all this discussion of being truthful about your limitations, it is also important not to allow excessive modesty to keep you from being too reserved about your abilities. While faking skills you don't have is often a symptom of arrogance, what most people don't realize is that seeing yourself as less capable than you really are is just another form of ego, albeit in the opposite direction. Real humility is seeing things exactly as they are, no better and no worse. Thus, being honest about your abilities also requires sharing the whole truth about your accomplishments, however uncomfortable that may make those of you with low self-esteem or a bashful nature.

Everyone likes being treated with respect. Telling someone the truth shows him that you respect him and his intelligence. And that you respect yourself enough to realize that you don't need to fake your skills to get ahead. Treating your colleagues with respect immediately starts building a relationship of trust. In the world of business, trust is a rare, and highly valuable, character trait. Trust will not only bring you rewarding personal experiences amongst your colleagues, but it will help you build a reputation that will bring you promotions, job opportunities, coveted assignments and infinite potential for professional growth.

Sound Honest

Unfortunately, it is not always enough to be honest. In brief interactions, like interviews, sometimes it is necessary to provide more obvious cues to others about your honesty. You can do this with proper verbal communication and body language. In Key #17, *Interviewing,* we'll consider body language cues in more detail. For now, let's focus on verbal techniques. Even deeply honest people can come across as shifty or unreliable because they unwittingly give off the wrong subtle cues when they are interacting with others. Our manner of speaking can give others the impression we are not forthcoming, even though we may be very genuine in our intent.

I know a gifted artist who is not a native English speaker. I've witnessed situations where someone will ask him if he can paint a particular image and, despite the fact that he could paint the image in his sleep, invariably he answers, "Practically, yes." Now, to the average person, this answer makes you seriously doubt him. "Practically, yes." What does that mean exactly? He can kind of paint it? Maybe? To him, the word "practically" makes his "yes" more emphatic. To everyone else, it's the opposite. I finally explained this to him and he now tries hard to be more succinct. "Yes" says plenty.

After years of interviewing people for managerial and technical jobs, I have come to realize that weak communication skills are not limited to those who grew up speaking a foreign language. Sounding as honest as you actually are requires responding to questions with precision, completely without hesitation. For example, if you are confronted by an employer or colleague about whether you have a particular skill that you don't in fact possess, the best course of action is to reply, "No, I don't have that skill. However, I do have these skills..." (List them and why they are relevant). "In addition, I would be very interested in learning the skill you are talking about and can start studying right away." The key here is answering "No" right away, then qualifying your answer. Most people have a tendency to start their responses with a litany of disclaimers before uttering the key word, or omitting the word "no" entirely in the hope that the truth of this will somehow be overlooked.

Employers often prefer to hear a candidate answer "no," but with a promise to learn and improve, because it demonstrates honesty together with an enthusiastic attitude – an outlook that there is rarely enough of.

This approach to sounding honest is, naturally, as important to use in every day situations as it is on the occasion of an interview.

Just to be clear, let's review this technique. If someone asks you a direct question, whenever possible, answer either "Yes" or "No." *Then* elaborate. It is so rare to get a straightforward answer. People are always on the defensive. They say, "Oh, well, you see...what happened is...I'm glad you asked that, but the thing is..." In the case of an interview your inability to provide a direct answer makes people, whose own continued employment may depend on selecting the right candidate, very uncomfortable.

In addition, be sure to make eye contact. When you are speaking with someone, don't look around the room as if you are searching for the answer in the pictures on the wall, or stalling until you can make up something convincing. Never start an answer on the defense. Be confident. You have probably given your best effort with good intentions (if you applied the principles of The Three-

Fold Path to Mastery), so you have nothing to be embarrassed about.

Instill confidence in your colleague by letting him know you know your skills as well as your limitations and that you are honest about communicating what these are. Avoid giving others false expectations that will only make them feel disappointed and disillusioned with you later.

Align your career, your reputation and your self with truth. Build your future with honesty, one right step at a time. Then, you will continue to progress professionally, to evolve personally, and to always exceed expectations – your own and your colleagues'.

Walking The Three-Fold Path to Mastery is about living life in a state of higher consciousness. With each action and each thought we seek to align ourselves with happier, brighter, more optimistic states of mind. Dishonesty brews shadows, aligning our thoughts with fear, guilt and shame.

One of India's, and the world's, most revered saints living in the nineteenth century, Sri Ramakrishna, could literally see dishonesty in his students. He said, "The virtue of truthfulness is most important. If a man always speaks the truth and holds to the truth tenaciously, he will realize God; for God is Truth." One of his close disciples, Rakhal (who later took the monastic name Brahmananda and became a spiritual giant in his own right) once told a small lie in joking to a friend. Later he encountered Ramakrishna, who said to him, "I can't look at you. I see a veil of ignorance over your face. Tell me, have you done anything wrong?" After a few moments Rakhal remembered the earlier incident and confessed. His teacher warned him never to lie again, that it would prevent him from attaining his spiritual goals.[ix]

Whether spiritual attainment is your goal or not, living and working with honesty creates a peaceful existence. With nothing to hide and no dark secrets to be discovered, you can go to sleep at night free of shame, regret and fear. You can always wake up to a bright day of new opportunities to serve your highest ideals and to work for the benefit of others, without the shadow of dishonesty looming in your awareness. You can devote your full attention and all your energy to acting impeccably and giving the best of yourself to the world.

CHAPTER SUMMARY

HONESTY

- Be honest
  - Being honest aligns you with the power of eternity.
  - Be objective and forthcoming about your limitations, as well as your talents.
  - Never, ever lie about your abilities or accomplishments, in person or on paper.
- Sound honest
  - Answer questions with "Yes" or "No" whenever possible, then elaborate.
  - Make eye contact when speaking. Don't look around the room for answers.

CHAPTER EXERCISES

HONESTY

1. *Be Honest*

a) Find a few moments to sit by yourself with a legal pad and pen, and prepare to make some lists. Consider whether there is anything in your past or regarding yourself about which you feel ashamed or embarrassed. In order to protect your pride, do you ever lie to others about this aspect of yourself? Add it to your list. Keep adding things until you can't think of anything else.

b) Long Term Exercise: For each item on your list, think about how you can address your feelings about this aspect of your life. Is this something that you have already grown beyond and you can allow yourself to finally let go of? Are you still the same person that this thing happened to or the same person that did this? Sometimes recognizing how different you are now can help you in releasing guilt or shame about things that happened to you long ago. It's as if it happened to another person entirely. If items on your list are more challenging, deeply painful or overwhelming, consider seeking outside help in resolving them. Like a knot in a muscle that a massage therapist can work on releasing over time, seek out a trusted friend, counselor or professional to work with you to release the trauma. If you are troubled enough by something that you find yourself lying to cover it up, it is vital to finally and bravely face it, work through it, and ultimately let it go. Otherwise you condemn yourself to the bondage and debilitation of living in the shadow of a growing psychological menace.

c) Short Term Exercise: Resolving difficult psychological issues takes time. While you are working through resolving items on your list that are severe enough to lie about, you can still practice being honest. Imagine what your life would be like if you were completely unburdened by these limitations. What if they really did disappear? What if they had never happened? What if they had happened to a close friend, but not to you? Try to go through one full day under one of these hypothetical scenarios. *Act As If.* If you can make it through one day feeling truly unburdened by your darkest secrets, try another.

2. *Sound Honest*

Practice your precise and immediate response technique by going through an entire day answering "Yes" or "No" to as many questions as you can before elaborating. Take it a step further and practice saying "Yes" or "No," rather than nodding or shaking your head, and rather than saying "Yeah" or "Nah." Aim for slang-free, perfectly eloquent responses without any hesitation and without looking up, down or around before speaking. This may be harder to do than it sounds! Keep working on this technique and soon it will become your natural way of responding.

KEY #4: CONFIDENCE

"As the activities of the wise man exist only in the eyes of others and not in his own, although he may be accomplishing immense tasks, he really does nothing."
–Ramana Maharshi [x]

Several years ago I was part of a team of consultants to a pharmaceutical corporation involved in a high-profile merger. I was in awe of a particular man who spoke with great authority, conviction, and admittedly, an impressive-sounding British accent. Whatever ideas he offered in meetings were met with nodding heads and signatures. It took me months to realize that the substance of his comments was only responsible for fifty percent of his positive reception by the corporate leaders. The remaining fifty percent was a factor of his obvious belief in the power of his words, his conviction in the feasibility of his suggestions, and his habituation to being taken seriously. This consultant perfectly walked the line between confidence and arrogance. He was a humble man, and thus, his confidence was extremely effective.

When I finally realized the power that his confidence conferred upon his words, it was nothing short of a revelation. We were being paid to share our opinions. What the company wanted from us was conviction. They wanted ideas and proposals that they could believe in, feel confident about. How could anyone take me seriously if I did not believe in myself?

The art of service to a person, organization, goal or ideal requires believing you have something valuable to offer, whether that is in the form of expertise, labor, or simply kindness. What you will offer is valuable because you will bring the best of yourself to delivering this service.

General George Patton once commented, "A man of diffident manner will never inspire confidence." He was referring to the necessity of leading by strong example. I understood from the example of my British colleague that regardless of the quality of my work, I would never be able to inspire others to have confidence in me, or in my work, if I didn't exude confidence myself.

Excelling professionally, in any industry or art, is bolstered by leadership skills whether or not you are in an official leadership role. Two of the most vital leadership qualities may seem like opposites, but are rather complements to each other: *confidence* and *humility*. Confidence is a deeply personal quality. It can be a challenge for many, as it was for me, to truly feel self-confident. The revelation that you may have something worth saying, that your work can and may benefit another person, organization or ideal, and the subsequent liberation from meekness that this revelation delivers, is worth striving for.

Pure confidence can only exist when accompanied by an equal humility. Otherwise confidence can degrade into arrogance.

At the same company described previously, we had another consultant on the team who appeared on the surface to have strong self-confidence. He had an impressive resume and wasn't shy about sharing his ideas with others. The problem was that it soon became clear he believed his ideas weren't just worth sharing, they were *superior* to everyone else's ideas. Lacking humility, this man's superficial confidence backfired. Rather than inspiring others, he made them angry. Rather than opening them up to different possibilities, he succeeded in getting whole meeting rooms full of people to cross their arms over their chests and glare. Believing his ideas to be more important than anyone else's, he became impossible to work with on a team. One month after he was hired, the client demanded he be replaced with another consultant.

A few months later we were amazed to discover that he had begun contacting his former team members, requesting we provide character references for his job search. Needless to say, no one offered to vouch for his team skills.

The line between confidence and arrogance can sometimes get blurry. Humility provides clarity. A truly confident person can be open to all possibilities and suggestions, because he has nothing to lose or to prove. Superficial confidence can arise from feeling that you are better than others, more important than others, more intelligent, more capable, or somehow more worthy of respect. Someone with superficial confidence is threatened by the ideas other people offer and suspicious of their alternative approaches to solving a problem.

The role of any professional seeking to provide service is to offer guidance and expert knowledge to help solve a problem. A master is always interested in passing along information, sharing knowledge and, most importantly, in constantly learning. A master feels that all ideas are worth entertaining, even if at first they may seem unlikely to succeed. The arrogance of limiting outside input and the sharing of knowledge is like shutting a window and pulling down the blinds. You cut off all possibility of light shining in.

A university professor went to see a Zen master in his home. The professor began to talk all about Zen while the master silently poured tea into the professor's cup. The professor kept talking and the master continued to pour tea until the tea began flowing out of the cup, onto the table and then the floor. "What are you doing?" the professor cried. The master said, "You are like this cup. How can you learn anything until you first empty your cup?"

As the appointed person in your role, you are the expert. However, there will come times when your colleagues or even non-experts on a subject are able to shed light on a problem. Just because someone makes a comment or provides a solution that you didn't think of or that you didn't offer first, doesn't invalidate your ability to do your job. Too many times I have witnessed one person shutting down (or more accurately, shutting up) a colleague out of embarrassment, when the "non-expert" or person of lower rank shared a novel idea. The interesting thing is that this makes the "expert" look even less competent. A true professional listens democratically to all ideas, since his goal is to find the best solution to the problem.

In *The HP Way*, David Packard describes the history of the $25 billion company he founded in a Palo Alto garage in 1938 with college buddy Will Hewlett. He describes an unusual and illuminating practice they initiated that became one of the foundations of their creative culture, and which was, according to him, one of the major reasons for the company's success. It was the practice of encouraging all employees, from the lowest paid tech person to the most senior executive, to share their ideas or creative solutions with management. Their Corporate Objectives statement says, "Everyone has something to contribute: It's not about title, level or tenure." [xi]

By recognizing the possibility that each employee could make contributions, they saw that they could draw from the creativity of all of their staff, rather than just the people in a particular department; thus, they could maximize their chances of finding the best solution to a problem. This approach empowered their employees and made each person feel valued and part of the team. As a result of this, and other enlightened initiatives, HewlettPackard became an incredible success story and the company has repeatedly won awards for being a fulfilling place to work. It remained on Fortune Magazine's "100 Best Companies to Work For" (compiled by Fortune and the Great Places to Work Institute) for the first four years the list was produced, dropping out only after their merger with Compaq in 2002.

The founders of HewlettPackard realized what wise people have throughout history: that no one person on this planet has all the answers, and that each person contains within himself the potential to be brilliant, heroic, loving, kind and strong. Everyone has an innate perfection – the same perfection that we see in the rhythms of all of nature. Waves rise up continuously from the sea, travel their course, regenerate, and wash against the shoreline. The sun rises and sets, perfectly, forever. Birds fly south in the winter, salmon swim upstream to lay their eggs, flowers bloom and give their seeds to the wind, clouds form and water the earth with rain, volcanoes spit fire from the earth's core, the moon revolves around the earth and the earth around the sun. We don't need to know the scientific details of all these natural occurrences to see the perfection of the greater whole – how all things arise and pass away in the continuous symphony of the universe. Try to remember that each individual you encounter is part of this natural symphony and has at least the *potential* to touch inspiration.

Confident people react to a suggestion with openness, kindness and gratitude. To understand humility and counteract any tendency to allow confidence to turn into arrogance, think of being gentle. As an agent of change, your role is to effectively help others transform their lives. Consider that a change imposed is a change opposed. If you try to sway people with force – which is ultimately the same as with arrogance – you may find that you are facing a room full of people with their arms crossed, glaring at you. Treat your colleagues with respect and understanding, and they will trust you and allow you to guide them. By gently and humbly sharing ideas that you believe in completely, you can shed light on a confounding situation. With confidence as your strength and gentleness as the light, you throw open the window and let up the blinds of ignorance. Then, you can effect change.

Here is a lovely story about coaxing change effectively: One day, the Wind said to the Sun, "I am more powerful than you are, and I will prove it." The Sun agreed to the challenge, smiling wisely. "You see that man on the street there? I will make him remove his overcoat faster than you can," boasted the Wind. "Show me, then," said the Sun. The Wind drew in a tremendous breath and then blew it with great force at the man on the street. The man bent his head into the wind and pulled his coat around him more tightly, fastening the belt. The stronger the Wind blew, bending trees and blowing leaves around the sidewalk, the more tightly the man clutched his coat to him, refusing to submit. After some time, surprised and embarrassed, the Wind admitted defeat. The Sun offered to try to get the man to remove his overcoat. The Wind laughed, and said, "Try if you can, silly Sun." The Sun smiled down at the man, showering him with warm rays of light. The Sun moved all the clouds aside and warmed the Earth. The man looked up at the sky, the clouds gone, and smiled at the Sun. After just a few minutes, he unfastened his coat and removed it, draping it over his arm.

Gentleness can be even more powerful than force. Gentleness is a quality of humility. Only someone with humility can truly be confident.

If you strive always to do better, to hold yourself to a higher ethical standard, continue to learn new things all the time, and treat others with respect, your confidence will come naturally and your power to guide others to success will emerge.

CHAPTER SUMMARY

CONFIDENCE

- You must have self-confidence in order to inspire others to have confidence in you.
- A confident person has nothing to lose, and nothing to prove. Respect others and their innate perfection as part of nature. Be open to all suggestions and offers of assistance.
- Agents of change must be leaders, by example, even if not by role.
- People with superficial confidence are arrogant. True confidence requires humility.
- Gentleness can help you understand humility. Change is more likely when inspired by gentleness, rather than force.

CHAPTER EXERCISES

CONFIDENCE

1. *Understanding Confidence*

Do you know what real confidence feels like? Let's find out. In Key #3, *Honesty*, we learned that humility is *seeing things exactly as they are, no better and no worse*. And in this Key we learned that real confidence is intertwined with humility. Thus, we can understand that Confidence is an expression of Truth. Of course, that is why you can believe in it and why you can inspire others to believe in you – because if you are confident and humble, then you are speaking the truth. To understand what real confidence feels like, we'll do a very simple exercise.

a) Answer this question: What color hair do you have? Look in the mirror and come up with some adjectives to describe your hair.

b) Now ask someone to pose the question to you, "What color hair do you have?" Answer them.

While you were speaking, did you doubt yourself? Did you believe completely in the veracity of your response? That is what confidence feels like, when it is not corrupted by arrogance. It simply sounds like the truth. It is something you can speak about with conviction and honesty.

2. *Understanding Gentleness*

The next time you want to convince someone to take your opinion, try taking the approach that top salespeople and marketers use to convince us to buy their products: rather than trying to aggressively force someone to see your side of things, try to help them see what's in it for them. What makes your idea create a better scenario for them than an alternative one? Try this out tomorrow:

a) Wait for an opportunity to present itself, where someone asks you for your opinion about how to solve a problem or about a choice to make. Before you offer your advice, consider carefully how the outcome will affect the person you are speaking with. Imagine yourself in his place.

b) Forgetting for a moment what outcome you are hoping for personally, describe the benefits of your solution from the perspective of your colleague. Rather than trying to *impose* upon him your solution from your point of view, paint a picture for him that he will understand and appreciate, the picture he would see from his vantage point.

Key #5: Loyalty

"As they prepared to engage the enemy, a fragmentation grenade was thrown into the midst of the patrol. Fully aware of the danger to his comrades, Sp4c. Baca unhesitatingly, and with complete disregard for his own safety, covered the grenade with his steel helmet and fell on it as the grenade exploded, thereby absorbing the lethal fragments and concussion with his body. His gallant action and total disregard for his personal well-being directly saved 8 men from certain serious injury or death."

– Citation for John P. Baca,
Specialist Fourth Class, U.S. Army,
Company D, 1st Battalion, 12th Cavalry,
1st Cavalry Division. Recipient of the
(Congressional) Medal of Honor,
February 10, 1970, for conspicuous
gallantry and intrepidity in action
at the risk of his life above and
beyond the call of duty.

In the treasured Hindu story of the *Ramayana* we find one of literature's most exquisite tales of loyalty. The ancient saga begins with Prince Rama of the magnificent kingdom of Ayodya, forced by his sinister stepmother to abdicate his claim to the throne. Rama is a great warrior, noble and deeply honorable. It was said, "Of all men, only Rama was born knowing his own heart." With disregard for his own comfort and despite the protests of the people of the kingdom, he allows himself to be banished to the forest for 14 years in order to honor a promise his father made. His pure and faithful wife Sita and his devoted half-brother Lakshmana join him on the journey. Mythical adventures with ogres and demons ensue. One day, the horrible, ten-headed demon king Ravana abducts Sita. Rama and Lakshmana launch an urgent search for her. Soon they come upon an army of talking monkeys and their brave leader, Hanuman. Hanuman finds Sita quickly. He sets fire to Ravana's city and then, with thousands of his monkeys, joins a fierce battle to return her to Rama. Rama is, of course, an enlightened sage and magical warrior, the "savior" of Sita, and of humanity. Hanuman recognizes this; and it is his unwavering loyalty to Rama throughout the story that provides the *Ramayana* with such heart and majesty.

When Sita is freed from Ravana and the battle against the demons has been won, Hanuman kneels before Rama. Rama honors him for his faith and his bravery. In gratitude, he offers the monkey a priceless heirloom made of gold and gemstones. Hanuman tears it apart, crushing the jewels in his teeth. He looks down at the pieces of the ruined bracelet, apparently searching for something. He says, "Lord, though this bracelet looked expensive it was really worthless, for nowhere on it did it bear your name."

"Then, with his sharp fingernails, Hanuman tore open his breast and pulled back the flesh. And see! There was written again and again on every bone, in fine little letters – *Rama Rama Rama Rama Rama.*" [xii]

Rama heals Hanuman's wound so that no scar is left, and hands Hanuman a gold ring bearing his name.

This mythical tale of deepest loyalty can remind us of the power of remaining devoted to a person, an ideal, or a worthy organization. Living fully requires giving our heart to our work, to all of our actions. With loyalty the mundane can become magical. With loyalty we can find spiritual ecstasy in the halls of an office.

Loyalty is a precious and scarce commodity, particularly in the business world. Like a horse-drawn carriage, loyalty is becoming quaint enough to make you stop and point when you see it displayed in public. In the marketplace, where selfish motivation proliferates, it is so unusual to encounter an individual who works for the benefit of others. Recent business scandals depict our modern corporate culture as a plague of people obsessed with grabbing whatever they can for themselves, no matter what the expense. It recalls the image described earlier of starving people knocking other starving people down in order to grab a sack of rice from the back of an aid truck. Where is the nobility in the ethic of "every man for himself"? Where is the belief in something higher and more important than ourselves?

Without a code of honor, to which we adhere even in times of challenge and fear, we are savages and we are sad, sad beings. Unfortunately, we may not see a dramatic shift in mass conscious-ness in our lifetimes. We may not be able to control the selfish behav-ior of others. But what we can do is be uncommon. We can choose, each of us individually, to be better. We can decide to be loyal and allow that to distinguish us professionally as well as personally. On The Three-Fold Path to Mastery, we choose to do what is right, because it is right, not necessarily because it delivers an immediate or materially measurable outcome. The only favorable outcome we seek is peace of mind and freedom from regret. It may seem that this often comes at the expense of instant gratification, such as a moment of celebrity, a sum of money, or a short-term promotion. As with wise investing, loyalty pays off in the long run if you are sensitive enough to grasp the power of a free conscience and patient enough to wait for the world to reflect back the rewards that you will receive for your noble choices. And ironically, success *will* come and it will be lasting when it does, because it will be founded on a reputation for unbending rightness in action that can only evolve over time.

There are three main types of loyalty that it is essential to uphold, and which will form the foundation of your professional reputation and personal principles:
- Loyalty to your employer or organization
- Loyalty to your project team, department or partners
- Loyalty to yourself

Loyalty to Your Employer

The person who hired you to work for him is your employer. In my case, I have my own company and essentially I work for myself. Many artists, writers and entrepreneurs are in the same position. Nevertheless, I still see myself as being employed by others. I have staff and I have clients and customers. From my perspective, they make it possible for me to make a living doing what I do. Thus, for all intents and purposes, they employ me.

However you define your employment, consider your obligation to your employer. A person, or group of people, have risked their reputations, and in some cases their lives, on your ability to do your job. If you fail to deliver, either in completing a particular assignment to the best of your ability or in acting with a basic level of professionalism, this person will at the least look bad. At worst, your employer could lose his own job.

Now we will explore how it is sometimes necessary to sacrifice popularity among coworkers, or social or political gain, in order to truly uphold the principle of loyalty. Often, being loyal may only be possible when acting with a selfless approach to the situation, rather than a selfish one.

During the course of a job, project or assignment, you may find yourself in a position where your employer is being criticized, contradicted, or openly condemned by others. By "employer" I am referring not only to the signatory on your paycheck, but also to whomever you report directly and indirectly. Criticism could arise, for example, in a simple interaction in the hallway, during conversations over informal lunch in a common cafeteria, or before or after a meeting when only a few people have arrived or are still lingering in the room. When a negative remark is made about your employer it may seem like the cool thing to do is to laugh along with everyone else or nod your head in agreement. It may seem to benefit you socially, or even politically within the company, to go along with the popular view. To be loyal to your employer in a difficult situation like this pays off down the road. Masters are not always popular; we just sleep better at night.

In Japan's feudal era a fabled class of warriors emerged as heroic and godlike figures. These warriors were called "samurai" and they adhered unwaveringly to a code of honor founded in service and loyalty to their feudal lords or "masters." Rooted in seven principles known as Bushido Code, or the Way of the Warrior, the samurai were admired and feared for their willingness to die rather than stray from their ethical core. The Bushido principles, or Seven Virtues, are:

Gi:	Justice, Moral Rightness
Yu:	Courage, Bravery
Jin:	Benevolence, Compassion
Rei:	Courtesy, Politeness
Makoto:	Veracity, Truthfulness
Meiyo:	Honor, Integrity
Chugi:	Loyalty, Devotion [xiii]

The most famous example of the Bushido Code in action exists in the true tale of the 47 *ronin,* or "masterless warriors," who avenged their feudal lord's death and then ended their own lives in a dramatic final gesture of loyalty and dedication that enraptured the people of their day. The manner in which they did this has inspired imaginations for centuries and the story was turned into a play, called *Chushingura,* which continues to be performed annually in Japan.

In early Spring 1701, Lord Asano was invited to Edo Castle, the headquarters of the shogun. There he was provoked by Kira, the shogun's chief of protocol, into drawing his sword inside the castle. Though Kira was not killed in the incident, the act was considered a serious breach of etiquette and the shogun ordered Asano to commit *seppuku* (ritual disembowelment). Asano died honorably at his own hand, but Kira was not punished. Asano's household and assets were dissolved and his 300 retainers (the samurai) were released, making the warriors masterless, or *ronin.* Nevertheless, the *ronin* did not feel their duty to their master had been released, just because he was no longer alive. Led by a man named Oishi, 47 of these *ronin* vowed to avenge Asano's honor.

After Asano's death, the 47 *ronin* set about dissolving their own reputations, in order to cause the very anxious Kira to develop a false sense of safety. For an entire year the warriors frequented illicit neighborhoods, became publicly drunk and broke up their own families. Oishi himself, in an act of incomprehensible sacrifice for a samurai, allowed his sword to rust. Once Kira had been lulled into false passivity, the warriors attacked, and after the man who had brought about the death of their master refused to kill himself honorably, they beheaded him. The *ronin* surrendered immediately and when they were predictably ordered to commit *seppuku,* they complied, dying together as one. The play based on their story ends with the line: "We have recorded here their glory, ever renewed like the leaves of the bamboo." *xiv*

Though it is unlikely that any of us, outside those who may have served in the military, have formally offered our lives to our employers, the level of dedication the 47 *ronin* upheld is still appropriate to consider, even in modern times. It is important to see this tale as an example of loyalty *to a code of honor* rather than as a suicidal pact in defense of a feudal lord. To believe so profoundly, so courageously and with such discipline in a way of living that you are willing to die before you would dishonor it, makes a life holy. Would any individual in pursuit of the highest professional and personal achievements *not* endeavor to make right decisions, bravely and with compassion? Not strive to act rightly and truthfully with honor and loyalty, as the Bushido Code suggests?

When confronting a relatively unthreatening situation in the business world of hearing idle criticism about one's employer, is it so hard to imagine oneself as a knight or samurai, pledged to support the organization or cause that pays your bills?

You need to make the choice in any particular situation whether or not loyalty calls for you to openly comment when someone starts bad-mouthing or acting politically against your employer. Don't participate in a group bonding session if it involves demeaning your employer. In some cases it is better to just keep quiet or leave the room. If you feel that your employer has acted indecently or illegally, then you need to take a different course of action. Confront him, and/or resign.

You may not love your employer, but by accepting checks from the company, and indirectly, from your manager, you owe them your loyalty. If someone makes any kind of negative comment to you about the person responsible for your income, imagine this comment was just made in reference to someone whom you love – a family member, spouse, or dear friend. It is unacceptable. In fact, everyone you work with should eventually get the idea that you are loyal to your employer – when your manager can hear you, and even when he can't. You don't want to get your feathers visibly ruffled, or walk off in a huff, or engage in any kind of conflict in that situation. Just be above it. Don't laugh, smile or show your agreement with the person who has made the comment. Just excuse yourself if the conversation is ready to end, or change the subject immediately without acknowledging the comment.

Remind yourself that the lasting rewards of loyalty are more important than the short-term rewards of being popular. Rise above being concerned about fitting in or looking cool.

Have a personal code of ethics that you refuse to compromise. Your enduring self-respect is more valuable than any approval you might gain from a moment of social ingratiation.

It is best to be very discriminating from the outset – starting with the interview process – with whom you choose to work for. For a master of The Three-Fold Path, accepting employment means presenting yourself in service to a person and to a company. Don't work for people whom you cannot find some way to service with a clear conscience.

Loyalty to Your Project, Team or Department

Once you are on assignment, you are inseparable and indistinguishable from your work. Your coworkers are an extension of your work. Depending on your type of employment, you may occasionally be working on tasks completely independently. However, often, you will be part of some kind of partnership or team. If you feel that your team, department or coworkers are doing an unsatisfactory job, it is not acceptable to distance yourself from association with these colleagues in order to preserve your reputation. What you will cultivate instead is a reputation for being self-serving.

If your team needs coaching, try to help. If your team is hopeless, you may document this formally as a risk and confidentially share this with your immediate manager. You shouldn't blame all failure on others, nor should you claim all the responsibility for success when your team does well. On the other hand when you single someone out as having done a superior job regardless of your own input, this, in fact, makes you shine more than grabbing all the kudos for yourself. When you stand by your team, through ups and downs, you improve your reputation regardless of the success of any particular project.

Michael Jordan is an undisputed star and was often the center of attention on the basketball court when he played. During his celebrated career, he played on six NBA championship teams, won five MVP awards and was selected to twelve all-star games. Nevertheless, whenever Michael Jordan would get singled out for his on-court heroics, he always made sure to compliment his team. Though the post-game replays of him flying through the air – in a way that anyone watching would swear was not humanly possible – were hard to ignore, Jordan would assure his interviewers that the Bulls' or the Wizards' success was a team effort. He was quoted saying, "Talent wins games, but teamwork and intelligence win championships." He highlighted his team's contributions even when sports fans suspected that that was not always true, that Jordan had, at least once in a while, single-handedly brought the team to victory. Did this open display of humility and loyalty detract at all from Michael Jordan's success? Of course not. It just gave everyone a hundred times more respect for him as an athlete, as a team player, and as a person.

Loyalty to Yourself

Loyalty to yourself is the most challenging and also the most important of all types of loyalty. The hardest part about being loyal to yourself is understanding what that means in the first place. Who are you? Do you really know? Have you ever stopped to reflect, deeply, on what you believe in? What is ethical, for you? Where do you personally draw the line between what is right and what is not? What does being noble mean to you? What qualities are the most valuable in a human being? Which qualities do you admire most in others? Which qualities do you respect most in principle?

Take a quiet moment, or a weekend, and think about each of these questions. You may want to write down the answers. Write a biography of an imaginary person that you would most admire and want to be like. That is who you are! Now you simply must have the courage, the strength and the will to be loyal to that image. It doesn't matter what you were like before you did this exercise. It doesn't matter who you were or what you did five years ago, or five minutes ago. You can change your priorities in a heart-beat, if you have enough will and integrity to make it happen.

Don't let other people or circumstances sway you. No matter how difficult the situation, always act in a manner that is consistent with your ethical core. Always be a reflection of your ideal self. When faced with a challenging situation ask yourself what your "ideal image" would do. If that is too difficult at first, then hold in your mind a vision of the person you most admire in the world. In an ethically complicated moment, ask yourself, what would the person I most admire do in this situation? Then do that.

As we have seen, there may come times when you will have to sacrifice popularity for integrity. You may need to make difficult choices, to remain above the fray and risk being ostracized, in order to stay loyal to yourself. The rewards of these choices are lofty: peace, contentment, untroubled sleep. You can't be truly loyal, to yourself or to anyone else, if you care deeply what other people think about you – if you are insecure in your real abilities and feel the need to prove yourself to others.

Loyalty is beautiful. Only strong people with a powerful ethical foundation and deep inner confidence can be loyal. Loyalty is very rare. To embrace loyalty and live by its noble code, it is necessary to approach the world from a selfless rather than a selfish perspective. Loyalty is not always about what will deliver you the most immediate gratification and material rewards. Loyalty is about what is right, and what is right for the people that your actions ultimately affect.

How can you be more loyal? How can you change? By *Acting As If* you already are more loyal. We can become so burdened by an idea of ourselves that we perpetuate habits and weaknesses of character that we could let go of in an instant. Forget about any previous idea you had of yourself and start living as the person you most want to be. *Now.*

Loyalty is a 24-by-7 activity. It is a moment by moment choice. Living with this level of integrity will ensure a peace and freedom beyond anything you may be able to imagine today. Loyalty to oneself is what makes a person shine from within. When you can reflect upon a day, a week, a year, a lifetime and regret nothing, that is when you will know you have remained loyal to yourself.

In his book composed in 1899, *Bushido: The Soul of Japan,* Inazo Nitobe writes, "Bushido as an independent code of ethics may vanish, but its power will not perish from the earth...Like its symbolic flower, after it is blown to the four winds, it will still bless mankind with the perfume with which it will enrich life. Ages after, when its customaries will have been buried and its very name forgotten, its odors will come floating in the air as from a far-off unseen hill, 'the wayside gaze beyond;' – then in the beautiful language of the Quaker poet, 'the traveler owns the grateful sense of sweetness near, he knows not whence, and, pausing, takes with forehead bare the benediction of the air.'"[xv]

CHAPTER SUMMARY

LOYALTY

- Be loyal to your employer, or to the person whom you were hired to help
  - Don't participate in negative conversations about your employer.
  - If serving your employer compromises your values, find another job.
- Be loyal to your partners, team or department
  - Don't take all the glory for yourself.
  - Don't blame all failure on others.
- Be loyal to yourself
  - Discover who you are and what your ideal "self" is like.
  - Always be loyal to that image.
- Sacrifice transient rewards like popularity and political gain for the lasting rewards of loyalty to others and to yourself

CHAPTER EXERCISES

LOYALTY

1. Who Are You?

Loyalty to yourself is the most challenging and also the most important of all types of loyalty. The hardest part about being loyal to yourself is understanding what that means in the first place. Do you really know who you are?

It would be best to do this next exercise in a very quiet and private moment away from the chaos of your everyday responsibilities. For example, go on a hike in a beautiful park on a weekend, bring a notebook in your backpack, and do this exercise on your journey. Start by meditating for a few minutes if you can, or just listen to your breath.

a) Now, reflect deeply on what you believe in. Answer the following questions in writing:
   • What is ethical, for you?
   • Where do you personally draw the line between what is right and what is not?
   • What does being noble mean to you?
   • What qualities are the most valuable in a human being?
   • Which qualities do you admire most in others, or in principle?
b) Write a biography of an imaginary person that you would most admire and want to be like.

2. Being Loyal to Your Ideal

The biography you wrote in the first exercise is a description of who you are, who you can be, right now! For the next

24 hours, use every cell of willpower in your being to act in perfect alignment with your ideal self. If you can do it for just one day, that is the first step towards being loyal for the rest of your life.

KEY #6: IMPERMANENCE

"Work as though you would live forever, and live as though you would die today."

— Og Mandino

Despite powerful evidence to the contrary, most of us have trouble grasping that circumstances have a way of changing when we least expect them to, or least want them to. Particularly in the West, many of us have an unfounded optimism about good things lasting, while others have a persistent pessimism about whether their own lives could ever work out as wonderfully as they dream. Neither view is balanced nor correct; thus, with our expectations largely unmet, we can never realize the peace that comes from having a balanced perspective on life. This phenomenon yields a work ethic based on entitlement, rather than on a deeper motivation that derives from a sense of work's higher purpose, or one's own guiding purpose. Rather than getting upset about what has not been provided for us, we can and should expend the majority of our energy focusing on what we do have, all the while striving to perform our work to the best of our ability with the highest possible consciousness and care. This attitude will leave us happier at the end of the day, and with a greater sense of accomplishment.

Contrast this with the alternative: ending each day with a sense of indignance at what we didn't get for our efforts, and with the total absence of a sense of accomplishment, since we spent our energy being angry instead of achieving something useful.

In these days of giant corporate mergers (the year 2003 alone saw 374 mergers and acquisitions, worth $38.3 billion[xvi]), large-scale layoffs, accounting scandals and financial insecurity, mastering impermanence has become a necessity in order to maintain balance and sanity in our professional lives. This trend has led corporate employers and employees to approach allegiance to each other in a new way: both have started to abandon the practice. Stories abound of employers firing workers who have been loyal to a company for twenty years or longer. On the positive side, this practice has also reduced the stigma of an individual making the choice to work for multiple companies over time. The ideal of growing up and growing old in the same organization is not as respected as it once was.

While practicing The Three-Fold Path to Mastery will significantly increase the odds of your being retained by an employer, these days there are no guarantees of tenure. The feeling of professional fragility this work climate engenders can cause great anxiety. Let's consider for a moment the nature of a consultant's career; it can lend full-time workers some insight into how to deal with uncertain circumstances, and how to use these circumstances to thrive professionally as well as personally.

Although the nomadic lifestyle of individuals in the consulting profession may seem unsettling in numerous ways, one could argue that it has better prepared these types of workers for a life of impermanence and change, since consultants grow accustomed to changing assignments and office locations frequently. I understand that while a few unscrupulous consultants have to some extent tainted the reputation of the profession as a whole, consulting has at its core the principle of using expertise to provide service to an organization. Thus, I see in the ideal of consultancy an excellent template for all workers in any profession.

Despite the reality that consultants or other types of short-term workers may remain with the same company for much longer than their initial contract specified, employers still seem tantalized by the idea of a temporary worker. Consultants are contracted to do a particular job and then leave. The employer has less responsibility for overhead, training and long-term human resource issues. There's a great cartoon that shows the perfect consultant's cubicle from the perspective of management: with wheels.

The fact is that embracing a nomadic approach to work and the workplace can have great benefits for the individual as well. A good consultant is always ready to provide expertise and at the same time, to soak up information about his environment quickly and apply that knowledge to meeting the goals of his assignment within a fixed timeframe. In Zen the practice of being in a constant state of readiness to learn new things is called, "Beginner's Mind." The cup is always empty to receive. As Shunryu Suzuki writes in *Zen Mind, Beginner's Mind,* "In the beginner's mind there are many possibilities; in the expert's mind there are few." *xvii* Used to taking on new challenges in new surroundings, the consultant's consciousness can be more fluid, more accepting of the inevitability of change.

One simple, but surprisingly powerful, tool top consultants utilize to enhance their productivity and peace at the office is keeping a spare work environment. Like a wanderer, a consultant has realized that too many personal belongings carried around reduce efficiency on his journeys. Assignments can start, end or change on very short notice. Thus, wise individuals have learned to keep all of their files, both paper and electronic, in meticulous order, and to maintain a Zen-like office, cubicle or desk area.

The Tao of Desks

Maintaining a certain austerity in your workspace is not only practical; it is polite towards those with whom you share space. Glimpsing the neat and organized desk of your colleague while you are working, while you are walking down the hall or waiting for a meeting, is more relaxing than seeing papers piled precariously over randomly scattered pens, trinkets, dirty coffee mugs and frayed post-it notes. It's the difference between driving past a garden and a junkyard. Practicing The Three-Fold Path we aim to be as polite as possible, and to take every opportunity to make working with us a unique pleasure.

Maintaining a Zen-like workspace is also practical. As more companies reorganize and consolidate, and job descriptions are revised to fall under different department headings, it is fairly common to have your desk or workspace repeatedly relocated. I have heard reports of miscommunications amongst managers and senior staff resulting in desks getting reassigned without notifying the worker who used to sit there. When I was working in New England a few years ago, a colleague of mine actually arrived at the office one snowy morning to find someone else seated in his cube, with pictures of her family members neatly placed around her desk and an overflowing ivy plant perched on top of the file cabinet. His baseball cap, hanging files and various pens and sundry items were gone. Some of them turned up a few days later in the copy room near the tray of week-old faxes that no one had claimed.

Though my colleague had only been employed for a few weeks when this happened and hadn't yet accumulated a lot of belongings in his work area, he still learned the hard way that nothing lasts forever!

There is an additional – and, one could argue, primary – benefit to maintaining a spare work environment, aside from being able to move easily from one desk to another. A spare area lends itself to quiet, focused thought and productive work. It seems whenever I see photographs of the world's top CEOs posing in their offices, their mahogany desks seem to have nothing on them but a computer and an orchid in a sleek, black bud vase. These executives have learned how to conserve their limited resources of time, energy and available mental bandwidth for processing information. Clutter drains your energy. Your peripheral vision constantly processes the images of each knick-knack, stack of paper, photo, travel souvenir and free vendor-embossed ball-point pen on your desk and postings on your walls. Trying to focus on your work while at the same time subconsciously contemplating all of these tchotchkes and their associated memories will leave you drained and ultimately less productive. Instead, be strategic about your workspace. With care, you can still enjoy a few "homey" items in your area, while retaining your full mental capacity for excelling at your work.

For example:
- Choose a few, meaningful items to decorate your area. Avoid wallpapering your tackboard with personal memorabilia.
- Establish a filing system and keep stacks of paper items on your desk to an organized minimum.

By applying discipline to your desk, you will send the message to your associates and superiors that you are focused on work, and nothing else. Display the clarity of your organized mind with the meticulousness of your uncluttered desk. Here are some other recommended ways to practice the Tao of Desks:

- At the end of each day, straighten up your area as if you will never be coming back. (You never know...)
- File loose papers. Throw away coffee cups and empty snack bags.
- Take as many personal things as you can home with you that you've brought to the office (books not related to work, CDs etc.).
- Align the computer monitor, mouse, mouse pad and phone.

These activities will prepare your work area for the next day. There is nothing like arriving at the office after a beastly commute with just moments to spare before a morning meeting, and seeing your clean desk with everything in its proper and logical place. The very sight of that is invigorating. It may even give you hope for having a day of relatively controlled chaos.

On a side note, in the event you do happen to get moved at the last minute, you will have left the next person with a clean and organized workspace, which is an unusually polite thing to do.

At the end of each week, wipe down your desk, monitor and phone with a paper towel and the Windex someone always leaves under the sink in the bathroom.

When your manager or a company executive happens to stroll past your desk you will undoubtedly give them the impression that you are extremely organized, neat and efficient. You may notice that most other work areas and desks on the floor are decorated with some personal effects, from the extreme of the person with literally no wall space left unadorned, to the person with just a single family photo and a squishy stress ball near the phone. Try this: walk around your office. Notice the various states of array and disarray of your colleagues' desks. Do you see empty snack bags, papers, books, photos? How do you feel when you see a perfectly neat desk compared to a cluttered one? (Be honest: doesn't the clean, organized desk make you think the person who works there is good at his job?)

Use the opportunity of creating a Zen-like workspace to reveal your inner discipline to others. Use the discipline of maintaining it to further your own clarity of mind and improve your personal productivity amidst the anarchy of a busy office.

Keeping Your Ducks in a Row

The etiquette of keeping your documents and files highly organized cannot be overemphasized.

Conduct your work as if you will not be returning the following day. What if you get a cold, or there's extreme weather and you can't get to the office? You are probably working on at least one file or project independently from your associates. Is there perhaps a document, a spreadsheet, research or meeting notes that no one but you has access to?

One day, you will not make it into the office and someone will ask you how to get hold of a document you've been working on. Wouldn't it be impressive if you could direct him to a filing cabinet where all your files are clearly and neatly labeled in alphabetical order? Or if you could direct him to a folder on the intranet where you've copied all the most recent versions of your documents? Or if you could report that you download all of your current work to a disk at the end of each day, which can be found in your desk drawer?

In Key #16, *Concluding An Assignment,* we'll consider in detail how to properly close down an assignment, project or job. Some of this work will include turning over all of your files. If you can maintain order throughout your current job or assignment, then you will be way ahead of the game when your work concludes. By preparing daily for any eventuality, you will be able to smoothly and impeccably transition as quickly as possible, not just into another project, but also into a more senior position if one is offered to you.

Planning for your absence (temporary or permanent) includes:

- *Documenting all proprietary knowledge regularly.* If there is anything you have learned that no one else is aware of, this should be noted somewhere and made available to your manager or members of your team.
- *Training an alternate.* Whenever possible, if you have learned skills during your assignment in order to do your work – skills

that no one else at the company may have – try to meet regularly with an associate who can cover for you in the event of your absence. You don't need to hand over the keys to your own job. Just train someone enough that if you never returned, or were out for an extended period of time, no one would shake their head and curse the day they ever hired you. This practice will also pay off if you become uncomfortably ill and you don't want to have to spend valuable couch time walking your colleagues through your files in between slurps of chicken soup and bone-rattling sneezes.

- *Maintaining file back-ups.* Keep electronic back-ups of all key files in a public area on the network. Don't just store your work on a personal network drive that no one else in the company can access. As mentioned above, make sure that the files are organized into logically named folders, so that, if necessary, key documents can be located by someone without your direction. SM_2905 is not logical. StaffMtg_02_09_05 is.

Remember that any work you do for a company or organization while they are paying you is legally their property, not yours. Treat all of your products, whether these are documents, spreadsheets, software, analyses, reports and so on, as company property. This was likely part of the employment agreement or contract that you signed when you were hired. Nevertheless, this practice should be part of your personal ethical contract whether the company's attorneys thought of it or not. Therefore, make sure you store the company's property where other approved members of the company can locate it easily.

Whether you are a part-time, temporary or full-time worker, your professional life is invariably challenged by continuous change. Consider the martial art tai chi, which teaches the practitioner to become fluid, like water. Water can either be a gentle or a formidable force. Like water, you can gently mould yourself to any environment, any situation. Also like water, your energy can be conserved and stored, to be unleashed with devastating power precisely when and where you choose. Welcoming, rather than resisting, change you can flow with any circumstance that arises, conserving your energy and attention for use in accomplishing tasks and solving problems.

There's a great humility to the acceptance of impermanence. Embracing whatever circumstance you find yourself in, you can appreciate it fully, gain as much from it as possible. Living with a sense of entitlement is arrogant, and also impractical. Wasting the present moment consumed by feelings of indignance and ingratitude, you lose any opportunity that may have presented itself if you had instead simply tended gently and humbly to the task at hand.

The exceptional politeness of maintaining an immaculate workspace and preparing each day for the possibility of your absence is the only way to respect the privilege of being paid to perform an act of service. As an employee, consultant, temp, or any other type of worker, you have been invited by a company or organization to be a guest in the equivalent of their home. Tread lightly. Take less than you give. Share your knowledge. Accept change.

Sometime during the 1700s in Japan a young, unmarried girl became pregnant by a local fisherman. When confronted by her angry parents about who the father was, she pointed to a Zen master named Hakuin residing in the village, who was known for living simply and purely. After the child's birth, the parents stormed over to Hakuin's home, banged on his door and demanded he take the baby. Hakuin bowed to them and took the baby in. Though all his disciples left him and he was now reviled by everyone for his actions, he loved and cared for the child as his own. A year went by and the girl became remorseful of her actions. She confessed everything to her parents, crying about missing her baby. The parents went back to Hakuin and pounded on his door. "Give us back our daughter's baby!" they demanded. Hakuin bowed, and returned the child to its grandparents.[xviii]

Imagine the suffering Hakuin might have gone through had he protested the accusation that he was the father. Imagine the pain he might have caused the girl. Instead, he accepted his new circumstances and derived great joy from taking care of the girl's baby. When his circumstances changed suddenly and the parents came for the child, he simply accepted that his time for having the experience of taking care of him was now over. In this story, who among all the characters remains happy throughout? Hakuin acted with impeccable politeness, embraced change and flowed with it, and emerged better off than when the incident began, having benefited from an unusual and colorful experience.

Live without fear of the impermanent nature of your circumstances. Prepare yourself for the possibility of unexpected change every day. You will find that the discipline this kind of practice requires will transform you.

Others will notice. This type of behavior, this etiquette, will distinguish you. It is the steeper road, certainly, but that is the fastest way up the mountain. It is the fastest way to reaching the peak of your profession and to discovering the heights of your own tremendous potential for achievement.

CHAPTER SUMMARY

IMPERMANENCE

- Like a consultant, approach your work as though you may have to leave after a short time.
- Maintain a Zen-like workspace to promote quiet, focused thought and activity.
- Keep your desk free of personal items to indicate to others that your priority is work.
- Maintain a meticulous filing system.
- Regularly save electronic and paper files where they can be easily accessed by others if necessary.
- Share proprietary knowledge you may have with at least one other associate.
- Before leaving for the day, straighten your workspace. Once a week, wipe down your desk with Windex.
- If you live and work like this every day, you will be transformed. You will be prepared to reach your highest personal and professional potential.

CHAPTER EXERCISES

IMPERMANENCE

1. *Practicing the Tao of Desks*

a) Bring a camera to your office and take a "before" photo of your desk.
b) Then, even if you have a relatively organized work area, bring your desk to the next level of perfection.
   i) Scrub the surface of the desk
   ii) Empty the desk drawers and clean the inside trays
   iii) Clean the arms of your chair
   iv) File all the papers stacked on your desk and organize the contents of your desk drawers.
   v) Examine your wall space. Can you part with old cartoons you posted months ago? Do you have reminder notes whose events or tasks have expired? Consider replacing all these types of items with a single, framed piece of artwork that inspires or calms you.
   vi) You might even want to purchase a bud vase and a beautiful flower to decorate your desk.
c) Now, take an "after" photo of your area. Keep both of these photos on your desk as reminders of the difference in how your area looks and how it feels to work there. Perhaps it will motivate you to make the "after" photo more reflective of your daily office experience.

2. *Ducks in a Row*

While I recommend doing the following exercise for all of your files eventually, if you have not been maintaining an organized file system this project could seem overwhelming.

And that could prevent you from organizing anything at all. To keep it manageable, select a subject area in your work that has the highest profile and/or the highest level of interaction with your colleagues.

a) Create a folder on your computer for this subject area. Give it a logical, intuitive name.

b) For one week, make sure to save any files you create or use in this subject area in the proper folder or sub-folder on your computer. Make sure your sub-folders also have intuitive names.

c) At the end of each day, back up the folder either on a secure network drive that others can access or on a disk. Label the disk and place it in a desk drawer that is clean and organized. Assume you might have to direct someone to it over the telephone.

Remember, this exercise is just for one subject area, for one week. Don't look at all of your files and at the magnitude of the job of organizing all of them, and then throw up your hands in frustration, totally giving up. The best way to integrate large changes into your routine is to break off small, manageable pieces, one at a time. Conquer little battles first. Once you have gained control over a single subject area in your files, you can start to tackle the rest, one by one. Before you know it, you'll have made a significant impact in your ability to be and to stay organized.

KEY #7: DETACHMENT

"Far from each other, and leading to different ends, are ignorance and knowledge. Thee, O Nachiketa, I regard as one who aspires after knowledge, for a multitude of pleasant objects were unable to tempt thee."

– Katha Upanishad[xix]

Imagine that for every tangible and intangible thing you crave, there is a fishing line knotted tightly in your solar plexus, with the other end wrapped securely around the object of your desire.

Picture a different set of fishing lines in your chest with the other ends fastened around the people that you love and also the people that you despise.

Finally, imagine that your idea of who you are is a rock around which a few fishing lines are tied, the other ends knotted securely in your throat.

Every time one of the things you want becomes less available, you can feel its respective line tugging in your gut. Every time someone you love hurts you, the fishing line fastened to this person sends pain directly into your chest. Every time you are criticized at work, the line tied to the person you imagine yourself to be pulls taut, making your throat burn.

You are a marionette. You imagine that you are in control of your life, with your electronic organizer, cell phone and three e-mail accounts – but in fact, you are completely at the mercy of the things you want and the people in your life.

You are attached to an idea you have that you are good at what you do. "I am good at my job," you think.

You are attached to an idea you have that you are reasonably good looking. "I am not unattractive," you think.

You are attached to an idea you have that, since you have worked hard and try to be a decent person, you are owed a comfortable life. "I deserve this, and this, and that," you think.

Take nothing for granted. The only constant in this world is change. If you become fixated on any particular eventuality, then you are attached.

Releasing yourself from attachments is the only way to maneuver through your daily struggles without suffering constantly.

By releasing the lines that connect you to the things you desire and the things you hope to avoid, you will release their hold over you. When you don't get exactly what you want, when situations in your life don't turn out exactly how you would have wanted, when people don't act towards you exactly how you want them to, you won't be uncontrollably pulled or tugged or tormented.

How do you release the lines? How do you gain some measure of detachment from the objects and people and circumstances that you care about?

The answer is *with humility.*

If you have humility you don't assume that you are so important that life should work out as you want it to. If you are humble, you don't always expect others to indulge your every whim, and you don't maintain such a rigid view of yourself that any criticism threatens to launch you into fits of anger in protest.

Individuals who can remain detached are able to maintain a relaxed discipline as they conduct their work. Detachment ensures balance. Detachment ensures that your sense of injustice or righteous indignation won't flare up when you are criticized or embarrassed or confronted.

In his treatise on conflict and strategy, *The Book of Five Rings,* the legendary samurai Musashi Miyamoto teaches, "It is imperative to master the principles of the art of war and learn to be unmoved in mind even in the heat of battle."[xx] Sun Tzu, in *The Art of War,* also pointed out that being attached and emotional in battle is a sure predictor of failure.[xxi]

Detachment is one of the most effective tools for individuals who aspire to act with graceful etiquette. Nothing is less professional than losing your cool in front of, or at, a colleague. It is likely that you will encounter difficult people and stressful situations on a regular basis at work. The poise with which you handle antagonism and conflict is a measure of your ability to remain detached.

Detachment is one of the Fundamental Principles of The Three-Fold Path to Mastery, which also include *Service* and *Humility;* in this context, *Detachment* is about being present and mindful when engaged in any action. The point is not to become overly fixated on the fruits of our labor, but to conserve our energy and our attention for acting impeccably. This application of detachment relates to every activity we are engaged in, throughout the Three Pathways. However, in this Key, we will review the practice of detachment in even greater complexity, as it relates to our involvement with other people, possessions, ideals and circumstances, as well as outcomes.

Gambling your sanity and happiness on circumstances turning out the way you have planned or decided they must, you lose all enjoyment in the process of arriving at that end. If the situation turns out another way, you will have lost twice: you will have missed out on the fun of the journey itself and you will be unhappy with the outcome. The joy of working is found in each moment you are engaged in a task and in the experience of watching a project unfold. Parents describe with breathless thrill the experience of watching their children grow up. They take pictures and videos of their sons and daughters and make pencil marks on the wall to document their growth. This is relishing the joy of the journey. Most parents don't see their little baby giggling in the crib and spend every moment for the next forty-five years focused on their child being elected President of the United States. Of course, parents might *think* about that. But the thought of a particular outcome does not obsessively consume a healthy parent's world to the exclusion of being able to enjoy reading to their infant, assisting their ten year old with his homework, helping to select their teenager's goofy-looking prom outfit and so on.

Work is like parenthood. You enjoy the evolution of your projects and tasks for what they are at each stage of their development. You do your best to ensure their success. Nevertheless, how they eventually turn out is in some part up to nature and the uncontrollable winds of time.

Experienced professionals provide their colleagues with objective assessments of a package of work, the risks involved, the constraints, the costs and benefits, the expected schedule. While we can promise to deliver a specific piece of work, like a document, we should never promise a specific outcome of a project. For example, an automotive engineer can promise to design a faster, less expensive vehicle. He cannot and should not promise it will outsell other models. Better to leave outcome-guessing to the operators of psychic hotlines. As a professional, you should only promise to provide an expert and disciplined effort, within your area of ability.

This is the essence of detachment from outcomes. However, detachment as a general practice has many other applications, which we will review now.

Detachment is the ability to be fluid, rather than being jerked around like baited fish, hooked and powerless on the end of a line. With detachment, we can move gently from one situation to the next, reacting according to the present, rather than to some imagined future or to some past injustice that we won't let go of. We can swim anywhere in the wide ocean. Free.

Any attempt to solidify into stone the nature of our relationship with another element of the world, with another person or with regard to an ideal, amounts to nothing more than an attempt to control what cannot be controlled. Only an ignorant and arrogant person would entertain the fantasy that something or someone outside ourselves can be ordered in that way. All we can control is ourselves. We can control what we think, how we react and how we feel.

It is ironic that in our attempt to control people and outcomes, we end up being controlled by them. In our attempt to force order, to have what we crave and demand, we find ourselves all the more at the mercy of chaos.

People often misunderstand detachment to other people or to beloved objects, and confuse it with being cold and uncaring. On the contrary, detached individuals do care very much: about the people they love, about serving higher ideals, and about working with excellence and nobility. At the same time, detached individuals do *not* care one iota about two key things: what the outcome of any moment in time or situation will be and what other people think of them.

One spectacularly efficient way to ensure a life of misery is to care deeply what other people think about you. There are only two opinions that matter: yours and Eternity's (or God's or your teacher's, however this higher power is represented in your life). This is not to suggest that you should ignore the wisdom, guidance and advice of others. Certainly you should make decisions and take action based on all available information, also taking into account the lack of clarity that can arise from your desires and aversions, and which could unduly influence you into speaking, acting or thinking unwisely. Once you have determined an action is correct, go ahead and do it to the best of your ability. Let the office gossips whisper like bored old ladies at a church meeting. The universe will reflect back the rightness of your choices and actions in time.

In August of 1886, when the Indian saint Ramakrishna passed away, his widow and devoted disciple Sri Sarada Devi (known as Holy Mother) was distraught. The Hindu custom at that time was for a widow to remove all of her adornments and jewelry. Following tradition, after her husband's body was cremated Holy Mother began to remove the gold bridal bangles from her arms, and prepared to change into a simple sari without a pattern or border. (Saris are large swaths of cloth that are wrapped around a woman's body in a specific way, forming a dress. The fabric is often exquisitely patterned with colors, stitching and even jewelry.) Suddenly, Ramakrishna appeared to her in a vision. He said, "Am I dead, that you are acting like a widow? I have just moved from one room to another." Holy Mother left the bangles on her arms and remained attired in her normal white sari with a red trim.

The local townspeople gasped with horror at her ornamentation and whispered viciously behind her back. At one point, tormented by all the criticism, she tried to remove the bracelets. Ramakrishna appeared to her again and told her to keep them on. Knowing she was acting rightly, she ignored the villagers and wore the bracelets for the rest of her life. Believing in the eternal presence of her teacher, respecting his wishes was far more important to her than appeasing the local gossips whose opinion would only matter for a short while, if at all.*xxii*

Our faith in the rightness of our actions and our thoughts must be as strong as Holy Mother's was. We may not all have a teacher in whom we can believe unfailingly, or someone we trust so implicitly to tell us what to do at crucial moments. But we do have an inner compass, which, with time and adherence to a code of ethics from day to day, will become calibrated to recognize "right action" like an arrow pointing towards magnetic north. It is only an attachment to what others think and say about us that can spin the arrow in the wrong direction.

Remember:

If you have done everything possible to succeed, and you have acted impeccably, there is nothing to defend.

If you have really screwed up, the best action is to take responsibility – and then immediate steps to correct the mistake.

Never allow yourself to be emotionally dependent on the outcome of a particular situation.

Never become emotionally dependent on the approval of others.

Detachment keeps you from being a human ping-pong ball. You might feel very happy one morning following a well-received presentation to a company executive. In the afternoon, you might feel angry that a proposal you wrote was rejected by a department manager. This back and forth goes on constantly. While you may not be able to stop feeling the emotions, you can stop your habit of clinging to each one.

The next time you feel a strong emotion at work, quiet down for a moment. Stop your racing thoughts. Step back. View the emotion as if it were being experienced by someone else. Allow yourself a few moments of reflection before reacting. Imagine you are holding the reaction or emotion in your closed fist. Slowly open your fingers. Let go. Imagine the emotion turning to sand and then lifting away, disappearing into the air.

If you are about to send off an angry or self-righteous reply to an e-mail message, wait. Save it as a draft and read it later on, after the fire of the moment has subsided.

If you are stopped in the hallway and become engaged in a discussion that suddenly makes your insides spin and your pulse race with indignation, tell yourself to breathe slowly. Don't respond. There is so much power in silence. Watch the person talking to you. Listen to him with detachment, as if his conversation was not with you, but with someone else; listen as if the interaction were occurring in another room and you were watching it from the safety of a one-way mirror. Wait before responding. With time comes reason.

It is so ordinary to engage in conflict. It is so ordinary to jump when one of those fishing lines tugs at your gut. It is extraordinary to just let go. Untie the knot, release the line, detach. React with patience, with kindness, with calm, cool objectivity.

In this throwaway culture, where pink slips are as likely to be found on your desk as yellow post-it notes, a reputation built upon superior performance and grace in conflict will distinguish you from your more average colleagues who have less self-control. Humility and patience, detachment and poise are the qualities that will ensure, at the very least, desirable opportunities for employment. And an uncommonly fine, free life.

CHAPTER SUMMARY

DETACHMENT

- Imagine that we are physically connected by fishing lines to everything in this world that we crave, and every person that we either love or hate.
- We are attached to:
  - the particular outcome of a situation
  - to a particular way of doing things
  - to a fixed idea of who we are or who someone else is
- These attachments allow us to be controlled by other people and the unpredictable circumstances of life.
- Detachment allows you to conduct your work with objectivity and precision, rather than emotion and self-importance.
- You cannot control other people or circumstances; you can only control yourself.
- Being detached is not the same as being cold and uncaring.
- To be detached, all you give up is:
  - caring what others think about you
  - being fixated on a particular outcome

CHAPTER EXERCISES

DETACHMENT

1. *Discovering Your Trigger Points*

As you work on becoming more detached, it helps to understand your primary triggers – the particular lines that when tugged, cause you to lose control over your emotions and clarity. Once you have identified your main lines, you can easily recognize when one of them is getting pulled and use that recognition as a way of distancing yourself from your reaction.

a) Make a list of the arguments, blow-ups and sources of significant emotional reactions (such as fear, anger, frustration, righteous indignation, sadness) that you have experienced in the past two months. List each incident separately down the page.

b) Next to each incident, identify the emotion that erupted from the experience. Write it down.

c) Now ask yourself, "Why?" Why did that particular incident cause you to feel that particular emotion? This exercise will reveal intimate and perhaps long-standing issues that you have struggled with. It may also reveal to you that issues you thought you had resolved still linger.

Stay familiar with this list and the resulting emotional reactions you have identified. You have created a map of your primary emotional causes and effects. You will find that your reactions to situations are highly predictable. Whenever the cause is present (someone hits one of your trigger points with an action or comment), the effect will be that you will experience emotion X and will react predictably. However, this is the first step towards unhooking yourself from these lines and gaining more control over yourself and your behavior. The next time you are confronted by a trigger from your list, you will instantly recognize it as the other end of a fishing line yanking on you like a marionette. Recognition is dissolution. Remember this. Simply recognizing that your resulting emotional reaction has been hard-wired into your behavior will help you to dissolve the line. You'll have advance warning and thus the opportunity to choose to experience the emotion arising as a witness, rather than as a helpless participant.

Just as with many practices in The Three-Fold Path, it will take time to master detachment. Nevertheless, by starting now to integrate the practice of detachment into your daily experience, you will find that your ability to maintain balance and self-control will increase by magnitudes each month.

KEY #8: BALANCE

"It is always in the midst, in the epicenter, of your troubles, that you find serenity."

– Antoine de St. Exupéry

Reading the news lately, one could easily get the impression that violence has taken over the world. In the past few years we have seen the fall of the World Trade Center towers, the bombing of a train in Madrid, ongoing warfare in Iraq, assassinations and coups around the world, genocide in the Sudan, the London bus and metro attacks, and scores of other shocking incidents at home and abroad. Unthinkable levels of violence can make us feel a tremendous lack of control over our circumstances and bring out emotions and behavior in us and in our colleagues, such as inexplicable anger, irritation, lethargy and depression, that impact everyone's productivity and quality of work.

With our world in a constant state of flux, and particularly when that flux portends the specter of bodily harm, our sense of being able to navigate our daily lives falters. It's as if we're sailing in calm waters and suddenly pick up weather reports of a tsunami two miles away and closing.

In a post-9/11 universe, fear about our future health and safety is added to the swells of change lurking just beyond the horizon. And amid these waves of uncertainty, we can lose our sea legs and fall or, at least, we might grab white-knuckled onto the side of the boat for balance. Worry fills our minds and we have little attention left to spare for efficient and clear thought. Concern for our own well-being causes our most selfish and self-preserving instincts to take over. The art of service is abandoned. Balance is gone. But what is balance, exactly?

Balance is the ability to enjoy life, despite these swells of change. Balance is the ability to experience a deep sense of peace, regardless of whether you perceive your circumstances at any given time as positive or negative. Balance is the ability to be infinitely resilient, not allowing any extreme of joy or pain, or traumatic event, to cause you to give up your guiding purpose. Balance makes it possible for you to stand at the helm of a ship, and despite surging, foaming waves tossing it around like a toy in the water, throw your arms back like Leonardo DiCaprio in "Titanic," and shout, "I'm the King of the Wooooorld!"

Guiding Purpose

Having a guiding purpose is one of life's great secrets to attaining lasting happiness in your work. One of the deepest wounds that can be inflicted on our potentially joyful lives is for the question to persist, "What is it that I am supposed to be doing?" Or, "What is my reason for living?" If you don't know the answer, if you don't know what you are *supposed to be doing,* perhaps the problem is that you are waiting for an answer. The real question you should be asking, in any case, is "What really makes me happy?"

Now we will explore how to discover the answer to that question, how to learn what it is that you really want from your life, and how to set in motion the actions necessary to manifest your dreams.

Just as we discussed in Key #5, *Loyalty,* in order to answer the questions above, you may need to take some time to reflect on your personal beliefs and ethical foundation. What circumstances do you require and what behavior do you need to manifest personally in order to feel that you are living loyally to your highest and most ideal Self? Once you have discovered your guiding purpose and you are walking towards life's horizon by its light, when you discover what makes you happy at the deepest level and you are able to align your actions with your dreams, then you will understand and have balance.

On The Three-Fold Path to Mastery the underlying guiding purpose of any practitioner is the interest in working to help others live their lives and do their work better, with greater joy and fulfillment. Practicing the art of service fills us, in turn, with a sense of joy and fulfillment. You may find that your guiding purpose requires an aspect of helping others in order to make you feel fulfilled.

A guiding purpose is all-consuming. It is the compass of your heart, your entire reason for waking up in the morning, for living. It is the light that gets you though the challenging moments of your life. You will know when you have identified what your purpose is, because you will not only be gripped by it, you will also feel ecstatic at the thought of it. Your purpose may be a goal with a specific end point, such as "starting my own successful company," or it may be a general goal that is more a way of life than a particular achievement, such as contributing to others' well-being and happiness.

Yo Yo Ma, the magnificent cellist and one of classical music's rare celebrities, was recognized early on as a master of his art. Beginning cello lessons at the age of four, he later attended Harvard University and Julliard, has recorded close to 50 albums and has won 14 Grammy awards. In 1998 after decades of success, Yo Yo Ma founded the Silk Road Project as a way to bring together diverse cultures through their unique musical styles. Through this organization he discovers and sponsors new musicians that otherwise might never get to perform in front of more than a few people; he also lends his name and credibility to help launch worthy musical, artistic and cultural projects. He appears to derive great enjoyment and satisfaction, not just from having a successful career as an artist, but also from helping others succeed in artistic careers as well.

In the summer of 2003 I had the good fortune to see Yo Yo Ma perform in New Mexico. The concert was held at the Santa Fe Opera, an "open" theater with a ceiling, but no walls. The mild New Mexico weather provided a warm, dry afternoon with a light, almost mystical breeze flowing from one side of the Opera through to the other open end. Birds were chirping away in the rafters. Yo Yo Ma walked out briskly, bowed, and began playing a Bach Partita for solo cello in a chair set up all alone in the center of the stage. Unexpectedly, a swallow drifted down from the rafters and began singing and flying around the stage. A true professional, Yo Yo Ma continued playing without distraction, eyes closed, smiling. He seemed to be in another world. The temperate breeze together with the chirping bird circling around the cellist and the sound of Bach's masterpiece of chords brought the audience to a fever bordering on ecstasy. When Yo Yo Ma finished playing and the volcanic eruption of applause faded, he stood up, bowed and said a few words about his Silk Road Project. He thanked Santa Feans for inviting him to play there and then he said with great sincerity, "And thank you for the birds."

This is balance. And mastery. A lesser artist might have been distracted or annoyed by a bird competing with his playing. With his exceptional balance, Yo Yo Ma was able to serve his purpose and, despite unusual circumstances, derive his own peaceful enjoyment throughout the experience as well.

Your guiding purpose may not present itself so obviously and at such a young age as it must have to Yo Yo Ma and other successful artists like him. Rather, you may need to live more and evolve through your life's experiences in order to be able to recognize what your purpose may be. Underlying any guiding purpose is something that makes you happy. On that note (pun intended), let's return to the question I suggested you ask yourself in the beginning of this section: *What is it that makes me happy?*

Take a few moments now to reflect on this. Get a legal pad and make a list if you like. Call it a list of your Items of Freedom. Try not to focus on material possessions, such as having a nice car, or things beyond your control, such as being married to the perfect mate, if you have not met him or her yet. However, feel free to include on your list totally impractical activities that fill you with joy. Here are some examples: writing, singing, making people laugh, fixing things, helping the underprivileged or challenged, surfing, meditating, continuing your education, teaching.

While you may have listed one or a few things that you don't believe you could ever turn into a financially viable career, you may very easily be able to change your outlook on your work using an Item of Freedom. If one of the things that sends you over the moon is singing, then you can think of your work as an enabler to finance your dreams of singing. You can re-envision your work as a receptionist in a law office during the day as an act of joy and freedom, because the job makes it possible for you to rent two hours in a recording studio at night to sing your heart out.

When work becomes stressful, you can allow your mind to settle around your guiding purpose, like a butterfly coming to rest on the leaf of a flower. Settling around what makes you happy, you will stop fluttering about and live peacefully.

Having a purpose which overrides everything else in importance can give you a sense of perspective when difficult times are present. Even when your circumstances may momentarily seem too hard to bear, or when times are so joyous it feels overwhelming, as long as you can direct your actions and heart towards the fulfillment of your guiding purpose, you can steady yourself with this constant, amid the unending cycle of change around it.

With your guiding purpose for balance, you can regard all change with the wisdom of emotional distance. Change becomes nothing more than the flow of the tide, in and out forever along the shoreline, while you remain steady and centered and rooted in your untouchable and all-encompassing "reason for living."

Balance at Work

Your sense of personal balance will greatly enhance your ability to do your work impeccably and will provide your colleagues and superiors with the impression that you are a consummate professional, capable and strong.

When a company experiences sudden change, like the announcement of a takeover or a merger, or when a department experiences it, like the announcement of the resignation or firing of a senior manager, employees can quickly become unhinged. Sudden change, even as insignificant as a behind-schedule or undelivered product, can cause people to respond with feelings of shock and fear. Sudden change can cause a large portion of the workforce to become unable to focus on their tasks, leading to drops in morale and productivity. While I was consulting to an organization undergoing a merger, my colleagues and I overheard rumors that one of the executives in our department was going to resign that week. As he was the final sign-off point for many of the department's projects, the prospect of this executive's resignation was cause for concern and last-minute contingency planning. By the end of the first day of these rumors, work in our area had nearly come to a standstill. Everyone was checking their e-mail, whispering in the hallway and taking long coffee breaks, unable to behave normally with the shadow of the unknown lurking around the corner. When the executive's resignation was finally confirmed a few days later, productivity quickly ramped back up to normal levels.

Your tenacious sense of balance may not change the world. Probably, it won't...What it will change is your experience of the world and the perception others in the world have of you. As we discussed in Key #7, *Detachment,* it is a futile waste of energy to *worry* about what others think of you. However, behaving in a manner that encourages others to respect you and which, as a result, creates for you a more rewarding work environment, is perfectly acceptable.

Remaining centered in the midst of change does not mean that you are resistant to change yourself. It is important to be fluid and accepting of the inevitable cycles of the unknown. You should also encourage your own continuous evolution, personally and professionally. Remaining centered thus means that in the midst of change, inwardly and in your world, you retain a strong emotional resilience. Keeping emotions and reactions in control, despite outwardly fluctuating circumstances, is what it means to have balance. Recreating oneself in the image of one's ideal, changing inwardly always to reflect growing wisdom and fortitude, are also expressions of having balance.

Balance at work is your ability to show up at the office every day with a smile on your face regardless of what is going on in your own life, and still have enough energy available for things like helping a colleague get through a stressful presentation to the executive officers. Balance at work is the ability to arrive at what you thought was your desk one Monday morning, find someone else comfortably stationed there with all of your things discarded, and not lose your cool. Balance at work is having an argument with your romantic partner just before leaving home, and not letting on to anyone at the office that it is not a great day.

Over time your steady nature will become apparent to your colleagues. They will notice that you are always competent, professional and friendly, and that your moods do not swing up and down at random. They will notice how you are always interested in hearing about their stories and ready to honor their gripes, but that you don't talk too much about yourself. They will notice that despite how hectic things have been, your desk is always clean and uncluttered and that you carry yourself with confidence and a quiet power.

Your balance will distinguish you, make you memorable and appreciated. No matter what happens, you will leave the office each day unburdened by regret, having brought the best of yourself to every moment of your time at work.

These are some of the profound rewards of walking The Three-Fold Path to Mastery: balance, loyalty to a guiding purpose, and a life lived without regret.

CHAPTER SUMMARY

BALANCE

- Balance is the ability to enjoy life, despite the turbulence.
- Having a guiding purpose is one of the keys to achieving lasting happiness.
- Having balance means keeping emotions and reactions in control, despite outwardly fluctuating circumstances.
- Demonstrating balance at work will earn you recognition as a consummate professional and allow you to leave the office each day unburdened by regret.

CHAPTER EXERCISES

BALANCE

1. *Discovering Your Items of Freedom*

a) *What is it that makes you happy?* Take a few moments to reflect on this.

b) Get a legal pad and write at the top "My Items of Freedom." Make a list of the things that bring you the greatest joy. As suggested in this chapter, try not to focus on material possessions, such as having a nice car; or things beyond your control, such as being married to the perfect mate, if you have not met him or her yet. However, feel free to include on your list totally impractical activities that make you happy. Here are some of the examples we considered: writing, singing, making people laugh, fixing things, helping the underprivileged or challenged, surfing, meditating, continuing your education, teaching.

2. *How Your Items Can Set You Free*

a) Prioritize the items and then rewrite the list, starting with the things that make you the happiest at the top of the page.

b) For each of the top five items, consider how you might bring these activities or ideals into your daily life. For example, if your items included "helping children," look for charities that you can donate money to, as well as volunteer your time, to make this item real for you. Don't allow yourself to be negative. For almost anything you might put on your list, there will be some way to access it in your life.

c) Look at your top five items again and think about how you can modify your perspective on your current work to reflect these goals.

   i) Does your job provide you with the income you need to finance a favorite hobby?

   ii) Does your job give you access to people whose lives you seek to improve through your work?

   iii) Does your job provide you with the cultural, social or technical education that will further your long-term goals?

   iv) Answer these questions, in writing, for each of the top five items on your list, or for more of them. Explain specifically *how* your job brings you closer to the things that you love or that make you happy.

3. *Identifying Your Guiding Purpose*

First, let's review this topic from the chapter. Your guiding purpose will be all-consuming. It will become your entire reason for waking up in the morning, for living itself. It will be the light that gets you though the challenging moments of your life. You will know when you have identified what your purpose is, because you will not only be gripped by it, you will also feel ecstatic at the thought of it. Your purpose may be a goal with a specific end point, such as "being in peak physical condition;" or, it may be a general goal that is more a way of life than a particular achievement, such as "developing a higher consciousness."

a) Hopefully, the previous exercise gave you insight into what your life's guiding purpose may be. You may have discovered that the more profound things that make you happy are all related in some significant way. You may also have discovered that satisfying your top five Items of Freedom follows the same theme. This theme is your guiding purpose.

b) Here are some examples of a guiding purpose. Do you recognize any of the ones listed here as your own? Do you identify with more than one?

   i) Contributing to the happiness and well-being of others.

   ii) Helping to save the planet ecologically.

   iii) Attaining enlightenment.

   iv) Making millions of dollars. (Don't scoff at this one. If it is your guiding purpose, be honest about that. Go ahead and make your millions. Once you have achieved that goal, you can go back to this exercise and look for another transformational goal.)

   v) Feeding the hungry. Helping the destitute.

   vi) Saving lives.

   vii) Contributing to others' education and knowledge.

c) Once you have identified your guiding purpose, you may discover that you have been following it for most of your life, one way or another. We almost always find some way to follow our hearts, regardless of how much our circumstances may seem to interfere with those goals. Keep your guiding purpose foremost in your mind as you work, and strive to fold more of your time and energy under its umbrella every day.

KEY #9: THE POWER
OF DEATH

"Everyone is so afraid of death, but the real Sufis just laugh: nothing tyrannizes their hearts. What strikes the oyster shell does not damage the pearl."

– Mevlana Rumi

A question is posed to both a worldly man and a monk: "If you found out you were going to die in one week, what would you do differently?" The worldly man looks out the window, his hands cupping his temples, and sighs, "Where do I begin?" The monk smiles and says, "Absolutely nothing."

Imagine the power and the freedom of living each moment of life without any sense of lacking that which you don't possess. It may seem almost impossible to have so much of everything you want that you have no more need for acquisition and no more need to change your circumstances. You may think, "Oh, a monk is simple and easy to please, so of course it is much easier for him to be satisfied with his life." But this is not the case. In fact, the power and freedom that the monk of this story enjoys is not the result of having everything he wants. The monk has simply embraced a fact of life that most of us choose to deny, or consider reluctantly with a shudder: the reality that are all going to die someday, and that none of us knows when that day will be. Embracing death means facing the absolute certainty of our mortal end, and the fact that it could come at any moment, any day. Developing the willingness and courage to face this inevitability might be the most positive, life-altering challenge you will ever undertake. It will develop in you a stronger foundation for attaining mastery, joy, freedom and success than any other shift either in attitude or circumstance.

Despite the obvious fact that we are mortal beings, the majority of us seem to have an extraordinary habit of acting as though we were immortal. We behave selfishly, taking no responsibility for our actions, procrastinating whenever we can get away with it, blaming others or our circumstances for our failures, and then acting shocked – shocked – when faced with an accident, serious illness or death.

We talk about death and illness in whispers. Death is bad. Birth is good. But embracing some parts of life and avoiding others doesn't change the fact that opposites exist. Death does not have to be bad. Birth is not inherently good. Birth and death and sickness and health are inevitabilities of life. Like rain and mountains, they just are.

We think, "Peace is good. Conflict is bad." But this is a misperception of Truth. Freedom can only come from perceiving the world objectively and embracing all her opposites as reflections of her whole nature: peace with conflict, sweet with sour, happiness with sadness, light with darkness, life with death. Peace is. Conflict is. Deciding one is bad and the other is good sets you up for constant disappointment.

We assume, for example, that spiritual seekers live in peace. Not necessarily. If they do, it is because their practice of self-inquiry and meditation has given them a deep acknowledgement of the fragility and transience of life. And yet, self-inquiry and the discipline of meditation can create a great deal of conflict: conflict of wants and wishes coming up against truth and rightness. So-called "spiritual" people are not peaceful because they have an uncomplicated existence. If they are peaceful, it is because they have taken great pains to face both the horror and the beauty of life with equanimity and they have attained a state of calm and a depth of wisdom that confronting these challenges can bring over time.

Having a complicated life with many responsibilities doesn't mean that you can't be a spiritual person. And seeking an uncomplicated life certainly doesn't ensure that you will achieve inner peace.

Judging one thing as better than another – or one way of life as better than another – creates confusion and delusion. Seeing everything with open-mindedness, tolerance and dispassion creates balance and understanding.

Wolfgang Amadeus Mozart said, "I thank my God for graciously granting me the opportunity of learning that death is the key which unlocks the door to our true happiness." Living and working in accordance with your guiding purpose, and with total immersion in the minute details of each moment, are the keys that unlock the door to a penetrating and lasting joy.

Living with passion and the acknowledgment that our time to enjoy and to suffer is equally limited, can inspire you to treasure even seemingly insignificant details. For example, if you are broke and you find $20 on the street, you will probably spend every dollar of that unexpected gift carefully. Let's say you decide to indulge in a small luxury, and you buy a cup of "designer" coffee with that money. Perhaps, you will savor it with more attention and appreciation, than if you were habituated to buying fancy coffee with long Italian names every day. You might sit down in the coffee shop, taking time to smell the rich combination of coffee and chocolate syrup and milk with cocoa shavings sprinkled on top. You might be thinking about the heat of the cup in your hand and taste the coffee with every part of your mouth as you sip it, rather than drinking the coffee absentmindedly while thinking about your appointments and friends and the cars outside the window.

Take a moment now and consider how often you actually engage in an activity, any activity, with your whole mind and body and spirit. How often do you read with abandon, losing awareness of the sounds and smells and beat of the world outside the realm of your book? When was the last time you ate a meal without watching television, reading or talking? How often do you walk down a street without being lost in thought, and actually notice the staggering array of colors and shapes and motion of people and cars and canopies and trees swaying in the dance of life?

Trying to arrange "perfect moments" for some future time, we miss the infinite moments of perfection that occur continuously, in the ever-flowing stream of conscious existence. Missing what is happening now, in order to plan and consider what may happen tomorrow, or to ponder what has already happened in the past, we arrive in the future having lost part of ourselves. Like accidentally dropping crumbs from a piece of cake we are carrying to relish once we get home, we arrive only to realize we lost half of the cake in bits along the road. Sleepwalking in an alternate universe of our private inner dramas, we miss what is around us, what is vibrant, tactile, rich and real. This can only lead to what may be the most painful of all emotions: regret. Taking time for granted, we lose the privilege of it without realizing it. Then, when time runs out, we feel the agony and responsibility of loss.

Have you ever seen someone die? I have. And I have spoken with other people who have also seen death. They all tell similar stories of the expression on people's faces when the spirit leaves the bodily form. So many people die with expressions on their faces of horror, surprise and regret. When a close relative of mine died a few years ago, despite weeks of illness where the family crowded around her bed and stroked her and told her she was loved, her face betrayed a wound no amount of our consoling could heal. She left with her mouth frozen open in shock, her eyes closed, as if shutting them would shut out whatever had happened to cause her remorse.

When something happens to slow our momentum, our endless pursuit of better, more, happier, we think, "No, not now, not this." We think, "Some other time, when it is more convenient, when I am stronger, wealthier, happier, then I can stop and appreciate each moment."

When a consideration of death or serious illness comes suddenly, the wheels start to spin. The mind reels with the weight of the undone, the unsaid, the done-badly, the said-poorly. We think, "Oh, I should have…I shouldn't have…Why didn't I?"

As we age, mortality becomes an inevitable consideration. For too many of us, regret is part of that process. We burden ourselves day after day with remorse till our shoulders curl forward and our heads bow in disbelief. Old age often demonstrates on our bodies the tragedy of the cumulative regret and shame of too many years spent sleepwalking through life.

I realize that I am painting a dark picture. It doesn't have to be this way. By facing the idea of our death now, with objectivity, attention and respect, we can avoid these indignities from befalling us in the future.

People have asked me, "How can I stop feeling regret, when I have done and said things that I wish with all my heart I had not?" The answer is complicated, of course, since you can't take back the past. Without going into the depth of consideration of each person's situation that would be required to right all the wrongs, I simply recommend this: fix what you can and start now, today, acting and saying only what will make you proud of yourself afterwards and only what you believe will give others a better day. Start now. Now. Make "now" right and the future will take care of itself. The past will fade into the shadow of the vibrant, multicolored present. Have the patience to seek the clarity you need in order to make the right choices, choices you can live with. Have the strength to then follow what your heart tells you is right, even if it is not the direction or the solution that may provide you with the most direct or immediate rewards.

The answers are always in the present. Ask yourself, before you do or say anything of any significance, "What is right, right now?" Then, be strong. Do what you know is correct. Make the choices during the day that will allow you to go to sleep at night with a clear conscience and with a sense that you have benefited the world in whatever small way. Have you engaged in at least one unselfish act during the gift of that day? Have you helped at least one other person to feel better about himself, brighter and more optimistic? Have you used whatever amount of power or energy you possess to give and serve other people, ideas or principles, rather than to gain rewards only for yourself? If you can answer yes to these questions at the end of a day, then you will have nothing to regret. In fact, you can begin each day with the same questions, using them as tools for guidance rather than subjects for reflection afterwards. Start the day with the intention to act unselfishly, to help someone else have a better day, to use your power to benefit others.

James Tryon, a Director of the American Red Cross in the early twentieth century, said, "If you would thoroughly know something, teach it to others." And if you would truly want something, give that to others. Don't let your doubts about whether you have power limit how you expend your energy. Don't let your perception of not having money or love to spare constrain you in giving out these charities generously.

By remaining aware of the preciousness of life we can bring more awareness and impeccability to every moment. By acknowledging the reality of death, we can live infinitely richer lives.

This is the ultimate act of mastery. How much more fully would we embrace this world of opportunity, if we were constantly, deeply aware of the chance we might be leaving it soon? How much more forgiving, patient and disciplined would our efforts be if we accepted that this might be our last chance to express these qualities?

What if we considered the possibility every moment that this action, this thought, this statement, might be the very last of our lives? Who wants to die having just had a vicious thought about another person? Who wants to die having just slothed through a workday, not really accomplishing anything productive? Who wants to leave this world with our own angry, mean words ringing in the air?

Alternatively, what if we brought the very best of ourselves to every interaction with our friends and partners? What if we spent our last moment on earth smiling with sincere affection at another person, or at the sight of a squirrel dashing across a tree branch, or at the feeling of the first few drops of rain on our forehead before a storm?

Since most of us have no idea when we will leave this world, we simply can't take a chance on not being in a bright, positive state of mind when that happens. We can't afford to risk being sloppy and wasting time at work. How can you waste what might be your last few minutes alive allowing old thoughts of frustration and despair to spin around and around, circling in your mind?

However, we can make the surprisingly simple effort to see the minutes, hours and days of our life as precious treasures. We can decide to stop taking ourselves so seriously and not get bent out of shape when someone says something or does something we don't like. We have a choice whether to be kind or snotty, optimistic or crabby, self-disciplined or selfish.

The choice is always up to us. In a teaching called "Mind," Buddha said, "Your worst enemy cannot harm you as much as your own thoughts, unguarded."[xxiii]

So many of the selfish, mean, sloppy things we do are the result of a false fear we have of not having control over our lives. While we can't control our circumstances, we absolutely do have control over the most important things that define our experiences: our actions, our words and our thoughts. In *As A Man Thinketh*, James Allen writes, "All that man achieves and all that he fails to achieve is the direct result of his own thoughts."*xxiv*

There is no person more successful or more at peace than the one who has recognized and embraced the power of facing the reality of his eventual death. You can have this power and this peace, too. In a moment of confusion or indecision, ask yourself, *What would I do if I knew I were going to die in a week? A day?*

If your answer to that question is a powerful response to leave your job, see the Champs-Elysées at night, Niagara Falls at dawn, start a family, race cars, write a book, or anything else substantially different from what you are doing, perhaps you should pay attention to what you obviously really want. Of course, you need to stay grounded and be somewhat practical in your choices. You need money to pay bills, cover your rent and buy food. You don't want to be selfish or disrespectful to people you love and disappear overnight in order to follow your own dreams. The truth is that you may not really need to change much about your circumstances in order to get what you think you want, and in order to feel happy.

If you honestly think about it, I would bet that you complain a lot, all day long, to yourself inside your mind. You probably complain about this thing or that thing being a drag or being hard, or about feeling trapped or powerless, or about being hungry or tired or frustrated. Like George Bailey, Jimmy Stewart's character in the movie, "It's a Wonderful Life," you can spend a lifetime thinking if only you had something other than that which you have, you would be happy. If you are lucky, you will realize that the secret to your happiness is right in front of you and available to you now. It was only your mind that made you believe you needed to have something different or go somewhere else in order to find peace. It was the distraction of this way of thinking that caused you to lose precious time, rather than life's lack of cooperation in giving you what you felt you needed or deserved.

This may sound silly, but sometimes it can help to make a list of all the things you have that make you happy. Go ahead – you can do it right now. It is often the people who are the most exceptionally fortunate that overlook their incredible abundance in the relentless pursuit of more, better, happier. I have a dear friend who fought in the Vietnam War. When he hears someone relatively well off complaining, he is fond of asking, "Do you hear gunfire? Are you bleeding in more than one place?" It does tend to put things in perspective when you hear questions like that, particularly from someone who knows what it's like to have bullets whizzing past him as he crouches next to the limp body of his former best friend.

We hear heroic stories about victims of cancer like Tour de France champion Lance Armstrong and teacher Morrie Schwartz (from Mitch Albom's *Tuesdays With Morrie*), embracing life with passion and courage in the face of serious illness and possible death. We celebrate their bravery and optimism, but then in a moment of frustration we forget that their lessons apply to us and we go and say something unkind to our parents. Or we do a half-assed job at work. Or we watch four hours of TV every day for months.

On The Three-Fold Path to Mastery, we make difficult choices. We choose our lives deliberately and courageously, by controlling our thoughts, by embracing the fact of our mortality, by treating every moment of our lives as a precious treasure. Acting with such care and discipline is not ordinary and takes work.

Practitioners of The Three-Fold Path to Mastery pursue a less-traveled road. As Robert Frost wrote, "...and that has made all the difference."[xxv] We have chosen to live with courage and fortitude, power and nobility. The things we must do in order to live this high life are honestly not that popular. Not everyone is willing to live a life of service to others, in a continuous struggle for self-mastery, pursuing the highest goals, intimately acknowledging the transience of life.

Unlike ordinary people, we bravely face the reality of our own eventual death with great joy, because Death will always show us how to lead a better life.

The exhilaration of appreciating our insignificant moments along with our milestones and moments of greatness brings contentment and a sense of fulfillment that annihilates the possibility of regret. The revelation of a free conscience makes you a vehicle for service. Unburdened by your own debilitating cravings, you can busy yourself with the only type of action that can bring lasting peace, and wealth and joy: unselfish work for the benefit of others.

That is why I say that Death has power. Because acknowledging it gives us freedom, the only goal worth seeking that will ultimately bring us everything we could ever want or need.

CHAPTER SUMMARY

THE POWER OF DEATH

- Bravely embrace the reality of your eventual death.
  - Use it to appreciate each moment of your life with gratitude and respect.
  - Use it to make wiser, more deliberate choices throughout each day.
- Instead of complaining inside your mind about what you don't have, try to direct your thoughts to all the blessings you do have that make you happy.
- Remember that you have opportunities to choose your experience of life constantly. You always have a control over what you say and think and do.
- Be strong. Only do or say or think what will make you proud of yourself or allow you to be at peace with your choices later. Consider that the next moment of your life may be your last. This is the secret for living life without regret.

CHAPTER EXERCISES

THE POWER OF DEATH

1. *Happiness Profile*

While you may have taken some time to reflect silently on the concepts introduced in this Key, I strongly recommend completing these exercises formally. Once you have a pen in your hand, your lists will emerge in more detail perhaps than they did in your mind. On paper the sight of your many blessings may surprise you.

a) On a blank piece of paper, write "My Gifts" at the top. Then, make a list under this title of every single thing you can think of that you are fortunate to have. Fortune is relative. Instead of comparing yourself to someone you may know that appears to have more gifts than you do, imagine life without any of the comforts you have and start your list from there.

b) Read over your list. Allow yourself a moment of gratitude for your exceptional privileges and gifts. In fact, this is a wonderful exercise to engage in every night before you go to sleep. Reflect on each and every thing in your life for which you are grateful before turning off the light. Try it. What do you feel like the next morning?

c) What is missing on your list? Write down three things that you wish were on your "My Gifts" list. Is there any way to give one or all of these things to someone else? To give them an element of one of these things? Try to do this for one week. The results may not manifest in form immediately, but they will certainly alter your perception of your world. Try it and see. Honestly give something that you wish you had more of to another. Write to me with your results (Mastery

At Work Success Stories, c/o Satori Sciences, 369 Montezuma Avenue, Suite #415, Santa Fe, NM 87501 or feedback@ satorisciences.com). I may publish your responses in a special section of my website or in a future book.

2. *Precious Moments*

This exercise will demonstrate the immense vibrancy and power of the world you live in, but that you often overlook in your haste to get somewhere else (wherever you are not) and to have something different (whatever you don't have).

a) Food Treasures

(Warning: this exercise may be dangerous for dieters!) Select your all-time favorite food or dessert and be specific: for example, your favorite ice-cream flavor and brand. Pick a day of this week when you can afford to indulge, and when you can spare 20 minutes of time without distraction. Go on a pilgrimage to the store that sells your indulgence of choice and do not settle for anything other than the precise food you identified at the start of the exercise. If you cannot find the right flavor or brand, pick another day when you can before you continue. Go to a place where you will not be distracted and take five minutes to slow your breathing and get quiet.

With each mouthful of your fantasy food, linger, pause. What does it smell like, taste like? Don't allow your mind to take you through journeys of memory or future dreams. Try to keep your attention focused entirely on the act of eating, on the experience of tasting, touching, smelling this happy food. What does it feel like in your mouth, on your tongue, going down your throat? Breathe slowly. Eat slowly. After you have finished your portion, don't leap up right away. Look around the room, outside the window. How do you feel? The next day, when you remember this experience, how does it make you feel?

b) The Joy of Commuting

On your next trip out of the house, either commuting to work or to do errands, eliminate as much multi-tasking activity as you can in advance. For example, if you normally make calls on your cell phone from the car, try to make the calls before or after this exercise. Eat breakfast before you leave the house, rather than on the train, and so on. Once you leave your home, imagine that you are moving in slow motion, the way movies show astronauts striding like heroes across the tarmac. What sounds do you hear? Listen carefully, as if you were trying to hear a child whispering from across the street. Try to identify the source of every sound you hear, not by looking around, but by sense. Take in the colors of your panorama. Saints describe being able to see life throbbing even in inanimate objects, like cars and buildings. Do you see trees or flowers or birds? What are their colors and sounds? Can you hear the birds' wings flapping? Can you see dew glistening on the branches or leaves of the trees? Can you see dried rain on car windows? Can you hear Mozart playing from a bookstore stereo?

We learn to tune out so much of our world so that we can pay more attention to the cacophony of the thoughts and worries inside our minds. Spend your entire commute this day trying to absorb every sound, sight and smell. When you get to your destination, how do you feel? At the least, you will probably feel different. We become so familiar with how we feel after thinking and worrying and complaining and planning, that when there is an absence of this inner activity we feel a strange void. Reflect on this void. Is it happy? Empty? Do you have more energy on arriving at work this day than on days when you allow yourself to think normally?

THE SECOND PATHWAY

THE SWORD

"I slept and dreamt that life was Joy.
I woke and saw that life was Duty.
I acted, and behold, Duty was Joy."
– Rabindranath Tagore

KEY #10: FOCUS

"Now when the bardo of birth is dawning upon me, I will abandon laziness for which life has no time, enter the undistracted path of study, reflection and meditation...now that I have once attained a human body, there is no time on the path for the mind to wander."
— from the Bardo Thötröl,
The Tibetan Book of the Dead[xxvi]

In Book XII of Homer's *Odyssey*, Circe warns Odysseus about the perils of sailing past the island of the Sirens, nymphs whose song is so intoxicating it lures men to their death as their ships shatter against the rocks along the shore. Circe tells him:

If a man come on them unwittingly and lend ear to their Siren-voices, he will never again behold wife and little ones rising to greet him with bright faces when he comes home from sea. The thrilling song of the Sirens will steal his life away, as they sit singing in their plashet between high banks of mouldering skeletons which flutter with the rags of skin rotting upon the bones. Wherefore sail right past them: and to achieve this successfully you must work beeswax till it is plastic and therewith stop the ears of your companions so that they do not hear a sound. For your own part, perhaps you wish to hear their singing? Then have yourself lashed hand and foot into your ship against the housing of the mast, with other bights of rope secured to the mast itself. Ensure also that if you order or implore your men to cast you loose, their sole response shall be to bind you tighter with cord upon cord. That way you may safely enjoy the Sirens' music.[xxvii]

While one could interpret the myth of the sirens as a metaphor for how a spiritual seeker (Odysseus) must seek to avoid the temptations of human life, we can also understand this story as a warning about the potentially devastating effects of distraction for any person interested in working at his peak ability. And since stuffing our ears with melted Tootsie Rolls from the vending machine and having someone duct-tape us to our chairs will probably not be the best way to help most of us to focus at work, in Key #10 we will consider more practical techniques for maintaining a strong, clear mind throughout the day, in order to work at our highest possible level of efficiency and contentment.

Perhaps you have had the common experience of innocently typing away at your computer when you suddenly receive a personal call from a friend who delivers news about an exciting party, a weekend date, or a future work-related opportunity. And the next thing you know, you are spacing out at your desk, or feeling your eyes glaze over during meetings, as you preview the upcoming scenario in your mind in ten different ways. By the time the day is over, you have barely accomplished anything.

The problem with this scenario is that it puts you in an ethical quagmire. You have just accepted payment from your employer for a day of work that you completed, at best, half-heartedly. And as we learned from Key #7, *Detachment,* you have also just lassoed your happiness around a future outcome, rather than finding fulfillment from your immediate activity. What if the weekend plans fall through? Then what?

As shocking as it may sound, by giving over a day of productivity that your employer naturally expected from you, lost in your inner musings, you have effectively stolen from the company. Even more importantly, you have stolen from yourself. You have stolen precious moments of living – fully, magnificently, and vibrantly – by trolling in a world of fantasy instead of embracing the potential of your own real existence.

If you catch yourself secretly engaged in imagining an episode of My Fabulous Possible Weekend, the correct solution isn't to write your company a check for the day you spent wandering the inner worlds, or to flog yourself on the nose with your mouse (at least, not too hard). The solution is to wrest control of your mind back from its dreaming and get it to focus on the real world unfolding around you.

There's an expression in Buddhist teachings called "mindfulness," which, together with meditation, is one of the most vital practices to master in order to attain enlightenment. Westerners call this "focus." Olympic athletes practice focusing techniques to improve and master their performance. The athlete who can block out fear, negativity, anxiety, personal problems, and even joy, is the athlete with the advantage. Later in the chapter we will look at specific techniques for adding mindfulness and meditation to your arsenal of weapons against distraction and against the poor work quality that is caused by a distracted mind.

Andrew Carnegie said, "The average person puts only 25% of his energy into his work. The world takes off its hat to those who put in more than 50% of their capacity, and stands on its head for those few and far between souls who devote 100%." Being able to focus one hundred percent on any given task or experience or moment in time, as Carnegie pointed out, will put you in a rarified group of a very few souls to whom the world will bow with respect. Very, very few people are able to focus with complete abandon on a specific activity. Attaining perfect mindfulness and inner silence is a quest millions of individuals throughout the ages have journeyed on. We hold those who have reached this level of focus on a spiritual pedestal and call them holy. Total focus may be a far off and lofty goal. Nevertheless, even the ability to focus 50% on your current activity will distinguish you from your colleagues, raise the quality of your work to new heights and bring you an unimaginable sense of peace.

With total focus you will immerse yourself so completely in a task – whether it is writing a document, chairing a meeting, giving a presentation, or just listening to someone explain to you what he needs – that you will become the task. There will be less of "you" and more of the pure action of performing the task. By turning off, or at least reducing the volume of, your incessant inner chatter, and hopes and dreams and feelings, you will be able to clearly see the most effective way to solve a problem or attain a goal.

As you increase your ability to be completely focused on one activity in any given moment, you will begin to see an increasing perfection in your work. Mistakes often result from distraction, and nothing is more distracting than entertaining dramatic fantasies inside your mind while you are trying to perform an unrelated task.

We've seen that focus is a form of mental discipline that few people can master. Perhaps you will become one of those few. Following are a few suggestions for improving your ability to resist the temptation of your thoughts' intoxicating song.

The Download

There are times when you honestly want to focus, but there are just so many things you've got to do. You have so many little details to keep track of and personal things that need to get done before work, during the day and after work. You may find that you are constantly making mental "to do" lists, shopping lists, lists of people to call, and other kinds of lists. Eventually, lists begin to self-generate inside your head all the time – during meetings, during conversations, while you are walking down the hall – threatening to completely take over your mind, like evil aliens descending in droves from a spaceship hovering above your home.

One trick that can lessen the onslaught of these mental lists is the "List Download." Set aside a few moments every morning to do this exercise. Write down all the little details clogging your mind; compose whatever lists you can think of in order to pre-empt concern about them later on. Type notes into your computer, PDA, or jot them down on a post-it or legal pad. If you make a habit of doing this at certain times of the day, you will find that your mind will eventually cooperate, and somehow the details will start to present themselves to you conveniently at those times, rather than periodically invading your mind throughout the day.

Once you have this list or lists, carry them with you. If you find you are mentally "listing" again, remind yourself that you've written it all down and that you can safely focus on those topics another time.

Multi-Tasking Is For Computers

The practice of mindfulness is a continuous process. You won't be free of cluttered thoughts overnight. Make it a habit to focus totally, completely, on what you are doing at any given moment, whether you are at work or not. Then, over time, you will start to notice the effects. These will include gaining an increased sensitivity to the needs of others, and a significant improvement in the quality of your work and the speed with which you are able to complete tasks. You will find that your comprehension of others' comments at meetings will be more profound, and that your ability to respond to questions and provide solutions to problems will be enhanced.

Think of your mind like the operating system of a computer. Some operating systems are designed to be multi-tasking: able to print a file, save a document and do spreadsheet calculations all at once. You can multi-task also. But inevitably, just as with most operating systems (despite the manufacturers' claims...) the increased load slows all the tasks down and makes each one less efficient.

Writers, creative artists and athletes are all familiar with the concept of the Zone. They talk in interviews about going into the Zone, where they reach a level of mental focus and inner silence that enables them to achieve otherwise unheard of peaks in their ability to perform.[xxviii] There's a transcendent moment in the movie, "Shine," based on the life of gifted pianist David Helfgott that illustrates an extreme instance of going into the Zone. We see Helfgott onstage, playing Rachmaninoff's exceedingly difficult Third Piano Concerto with a fire. The music is loud. His hands are consuming the keys of the piano, his fingers stretching into cords, his expression revealing a complete dissolution of his spirit into the moment of eliciting each note. And then, silence. We see his hands moving, his expression unchanged, but we are shown by the director that the artist and his Work have become so entwined that Helfgott has gone beyond matter and has entered into the silence of eternity. That night Helfgott played with perfection. There were no thoughts in his mind competing for attention with the music. There was, ultimately, no David Helfgott. His identity, his memories, his patterns of acting and thinking all dissolved into the perfection of silence as he gave himself over in service to his Art.[xxix]

We may not all be artists of this magnitude and humility (though we could be someday!), and we may not all wish to be. Still, we can strive to work at our highest potential by not attempting to focus on more than one activity at a time, and by giving ourselves over to our tasks in body, mind and spirit to the best of our ability.

Consider this analogy: that thinking while you are engaged in an activity is like a car driving down a road filled with potholes. Imagine how much faster and more efficient the ride would be on a perfectly smooth pavement.

Life Is Too Short For Boredom

Perhaps you have trouble focusing on your work, because your work is mind-numbingly dull. For example, you might find yourself in a lull between projects, where deciding whether to have the cinnamon bran muffin or a chocolate chip cookie for your afternoon snack is your big excitement of the day. Ask yourself, are there interesting projects in other departments of the company that you can get involved in until your projects gear up? Are there office-sponsored clubs, classes or discussion groups you can participate in? Don't be content to sit around and wait to be given something to do. People who succeed professionally have at some point usually distinguished themselves by initiating something useful during slow periods at work (though they often display initiative when work is busy as well).

Then again, you may technically have enough work to do, but find that your work is uninspiring enough to make the mating behavior of the flies outside your window seem scintillating. Consider looking for a different job, perhaps in a different industry entirely.

Too many weeks spent idly at your desk either waiting to be given work to do, or being tragically bored out of your wits, will soon turn your previously razor-sharp brain into oatmeal.

Schedule a meeting with your manager and ask him if he could help you turn your energy towards other activities for a while. Or, think about whether other areas of your organization might be better suited to your interests.

Life's limited moments are precious. Is it worth whatever you are getting paid to be wasting these moments being bored? In high school some kids might have thought it sounded cool to make money for not doing much. In the world of professional ethics and etiquette it is very uncool. If you are completely bored by your work – because you are between projects, overqualified, or you are not being given meaningful tasks to perform – you need to address the situation immediately.

In addition to avoiding boredom and the tendency to multi-task, there are two extremely efficient ways to improve your ability to be mindful that have been proven by spiritual adepts for thousands of years. These are Alchemy and Mental Fortitude.

Alchemy

Webster's dictionary describes alchemy as "a seemingly magical power or process of transmuting." This practice is very simple when applied to mindfulness and does not require magical powers. Here is how it works: If a thought arises in your mind that is distracting, change its composition to a thought that is less distracting. Simple, right? As people who practice meditation will tell you, trying to stop your thoughts through force of will only makes you focus on them all the more intently. So if thoughts start to flow while you are trying to work, don't try to issue some kind of mental command to cease them. That will probably backfire and create even more persistent thoughts. Rather, coax your mind to focus in a new place – or direct it back to the place where it was before it wandered off into la-la land. If your thoughts become negative or emotional, try to transmute them into brighter and happier ones.

For example, if you are typing up meeting notes at your computer and your mind starts to run through angry scenarios where you will be treated unjustly by a colleague, transmute the scenario into one where the same colleague smiles and compliments your work – however unlikely you think that outcome may be. Then, nudge your mind back to typing your notes. Try to get yourself interested in the words you are typing. Hear them in your mind. Listen to the sound of your fingers tapping on the keyboard. Focus your vision so the computer screen takes up your entire attention.

As the dictionary definition states, alchemy, like mindfulness, is a process. It is not an action you will perform once with miraculous and permanent results. At first, you may find yourself transmuting thoughts several times an hour, shifting your mind back to your current activity, again and again, throughout every day. You will find that after practicing mindfulness for a while, your mind will be trained to turn itself to brighter thoughts and to become still more often without your conscious intervention.

Mental Fortitude

Together with mindfulness, meditation forms a comprehensive system for gaining control over our thoughts, desires, aversions, motivations and the other distractions that prevent us from experiencing life in all its magnificent glory.

Meditation is like weight-lifting for the mind; it will lead to great mental fortitude. And the development of mental fortitude will allow you to exist in levels of inner silence and peace that you cannot even imagine if you do not currently practice any form of meditation. Meditation can be practiced easily and beneficially outside of any specific religious activity or belief, or as a complement to your existing faith. All spiritual pathways, regardless of culture or religion, reference one form or another of meditative practice. The art of becoming still, of stopping all mental commerce with the world for even short periods of time, is the essence of any realistic pursuit of success, either spiritual, social or professional.

Now I will walk you through a very simple, but powerful, meditation technique that you can try when you have five minutes to spare. This technique is not derived from any specific religious practice and is safe for people of all ages to try. First, try to find a quiet place where you feel protected. For example, I wouldn't recommend trying to meditate during your evening commute on the train, or in a room where other people are walking in and out. Find a place where you can be alone or where you can shut the door.

It is not necessary for the room to be dark. It is not necessary to be seated any particular way. You don't have to be cross-legged in half-lotus position on the floor. It's fine to be seated in a chair.

However you are sitting, just make sure that your back is straight. Take a deep breath and let it out slowly. Allow a moment or two for your system to slow down.

Once you are breathing comfortably, stretch one of your arms out to the side. Now, point to yourself and say, "Me." (Touch your chest with your pointing finger, as most of us do when we refer to ourselves like this.) The spot where your finger touches your chest is what we call the Heart Center. The Heart Center is not in the same place as your actual heart muscle. If you try this technique with a friend you may also notice that you are both pointing to slightly different areas of the chest. That's okay and normal. Wherever you have placed your finger is where your personal Heart Center is. Feel this place on your body.

Leave your finger on your Heart if you need to throughout this exercise. Once you can feel the spot without pointing to it, you can skip this step.

Close your eyes. Focus all of your attention on the precise spot where your finger is touching. Imagine your finger is burning a hole in your chest. Imagine that hole is a circle of light. Imagine that this circle of light is filling you with joy. Don't allow mental images or stories into your mind. Use all your power of concentration to stay focused one hundred percent on your Heart Center. Keep your breath calm and smooth. After five minutes, stop and relax.

After even the briefest or seemingly unproductive period of meditation, it is appropriate to allow a moment of gratitude for the privilege of the opportunity to experience peace. It is enough to silently say, "Thank you" before opening your eyes and concluding your session. Some people like to bow their heads or touch their foreheads to the ground if they are sitting on the floor. If you want to try this, just remember that you are bowing in gratitude, not bowing "to" anyone in particular. Bowing can feel warm and loving, as long as you don't associate this gesture with something negative.

If you spent your five minutes of meditation thinking a lot, then you may not notice much difference in your awareness. Keep trying. One day you will open your eyes and the objects in front of you will actually take on a new level of clarity. You might feel both elated and calm all at once. After just a few minutes of successful meditation, you will feel relaxed and better able to tackle whatever challenges you are facing.

As you get better at focusing on your Heart Center and keeping your thoughts quiet, you can slowly increase the time you spend meditating. It is important not to try to achieve any particular goal with your meditations – apart from calming your thoughts. Just enjoy yourself. This is a 5, 10 or 30-minute vacation from the chaos of your life.

Even five minutes of focus a day will produce significant and noticeable effects.

We will touch on the subject of meditation again in Key #15, *Warrior Training*. For now, just include the idea of meditation, together with mindfulness, in your understanding of how to achieve the elusive, rare and valued skill of focus.

On The Three-Fold Path to Mastery we practice the art of service to others, to the world, and to our own higher ideals. It is your responsibility to apply your expertise, your energy and your time in service as part of your work. Spending your time flicking paper clips into a jar on your desk, chatting on the phone or mindlessly surfing the internet is like turning on a faucet and letting fresh water run into the sink for days. It's a disturbing waste.

Working on a task while you are enthusiastically romping through inner worlds of drama is unethical and not conducive to the attainment of any desirable goal in life.

Seek stillness, clarity, focus and your consciousness will soar to new heights. You will sail safely beyond the island of the sirens and into the waters of fascinating future journeys, journeys that will be filled with colors, sounds and sensations richer and more magnificent than you can imagine now.

CHAPTER SUMMARY

FOCUS

- Allowing mental scenarios to play in your mind while you should be working is like stealing from your employer.
- Learning to focus is a continuous process of mental discipline.
- Schedule time every day to download your mental lists.
- Multi-tasking is for computers. Don't "drive over potholes."
- Seek alternatives to boring days at work.
- Practice *Alchemy* to transmute negative thoughts to brighter ones, and to return your thoughts to your current activity.
- Practice meditation to develop the mental fortitude required to gain control over your thoughts.

CHAPTER EXERCISES

FOCUS

1. *Alchemy*

For this exercise, you're going to simulate a negative thought, and then practice transmuting it into a bright and optimistic thought. This will teach you mindfulness and focus, as well as contribute to your happiness, health and well-being.

a) Close your eyes and call up a memory of intense happiness or lightness of being. Remember a particular moment in time when you experienced the feeling of being carefree, or when you were hysterically laughing, or when you felt truly peaceful. Remember as many details as you can: smells, sounds, objects in the room.

b) Now, conjure up an unpleasant thought, emotion or scenario that you experience regularly, and that has in the past caused you to become distracted. Allow yourself to feel the negative emotion for a brief moment.

c) As soon as you feel that you are authentically re-experiencing the unpleasant scenario, quickly shift your focus back to the happy memory. Put yourself back in that moment in time as completely as you can.

d) How long did it take for you to completely shift your mind to pleasant thoughts? As you practice this technique, you will become increasingly adept at leaping back into bright states of mind with ease and speed.

This exercise will allow you to practice transmuting your thoughts in a controlled situation. Then, when you are unexpectedly confronted with thoughts that you know are limiting your ability to function at your peak, you will know precisely what to do to stop them in their tracks.

2. *Mental Fortitude*

This exercise will help you realize how connected your thoughts and emotions are to the people you are around. This will help you gain much more control over mental distractions.

a) The next time you find yourself in a crowded place, try to monitor your mind activity. How much are you thinking? What are you thinking about? What feelings are you experiencing?

b) Soon after leaving the crowded place, go to a park or take a walk in nature. Try to stroll for a few minutes in a place as empty of people as possible. Now how much are you thinking? What are you thinking about? How do you feel?

You may discover that most of the time the volume of mental static you experience is largely influenced by how many other people are in your immediate vicinity. You may start to notice that right after certain meetings, more than after others, you feel depressed or angry. It is possible that you are picking up on the mental "radio waves" of emotional energy coming from other people. When you can start to distinguish your own thoughts and emotions from the ones you are simply picking up on from others, you will find it becomes much simpler to shut them down or transmute them. Gaining control over your inner life will give you a tremendous advantage when navigating work and personal challenges. You will be able to work and interact with others at your peak ability more often, and avoid the potentially debilitating distraction of negative, energy-draining thoughts.

KEY #11: POLITICS
& STRATEGY

"The Way of a Warrior, the Art of Politics, is to stop trouble before it starts. It consists in defeating your adversaries spiritually by making them realize the folly of their actions. The Way of a Warrior is to establish harmony."
– Morihei Ueshiba

In the late '90s a Fortune 500 corporation in the entertainment industry hired a Chief Information Officer to modernize their global technology and interdepartmental workflow. The new CIO brought me onboard shortly afterwards to create a custom methodology for managing and benchmarking technology-related projects. It became clear within weeks of her arrival that the three senior technology executives reporting to the CIO were each on a mission to get rid of her and end up with her job. Together with a few other members of the immediate staff, I warned her about the fantastic political maneuvering going on behind her back. Through e-mail, memos and coffee room gossip we were witnessing nearly constant scheming by these three really reptilian people. One of them would show up at the CIO's office like a comic-book villain, his hair slicked back with oil, European accent seeping over his lips like hot wax over the edge of a lit candle. Smiling sweetly, he'd compliment the major changes she was proposing in the department, although he was actively making plans to ensure she would never succeed.

This CIO was a no-nonsense, experienced technologist, with an impressive hands-on background. She wore practical suits, no makeup and flat shoes, an anomaly in such a glamorous corporation. Still, her team respected her. She got things done and she'd listen to anyone's opinion, from administrative assistants to senior officers.

Her downfall was not naïveté. I can't really believe that someone with her experience could have been that blind to what was going on around her. I think she just refused to honor the whole messy, mean business because she didn't want to believe it mattered. Yes, there were dark characters around, with their oily grins and fingers wrapped around kitchen knives behind their backs. But no, they couldn't possibly do any real damage. Well, perhaps that's what Julius Caesar was thinking right before he ran into Brutus. ("Oh, hey, hi Brute old fella, what's up?" Stab stab.)

At the end of the year the CIO was fired and Mr. Candlewax, who had been the most uncooperative during her reign, was promoted to take her place. Sad, but no surprise.

Understanding the political machinations within your organization is essential in order to be able to get your work done. I am not suggesting you play politics, though occasionally it may be unavoidable. I am only suggesting you become extremely astute: that you notice precisely what games are being played, and who the players are in each position on the field. Then and only then can you decide whether to become involved or not. Ignoring politics entirely just makes you a potential victim of the people who have chosen to play the game.

Becoming astute means that you will need to investigate and remain aware of all the alliances, battles and history between each of your colleagues and the history of each of the executives' and senior managers' rise to power. This may sound unpleasant and outside your job description. Politics may appear the antithesis of working with a higher consciousness as part of The Three-Fold Path to Mastery. On the contrary: as practitioners of the noble art of service we mustn't be averse to anything.

It's not useful to cringe about politics, just as it's unproductive to become angry when others disagree with you or to preen when they throw roses at your feet. Politics are. Acknowledge them. Cock your head to one side and observe them like you are watching a National Geographic special on raccoons in the wild. Put your fingers to your chin and in your best English accent say, "How fascinating." Watching the habits of wild animals doesn't exactly get you fired up with emotion, and yet you can get into the science of it and find it educational. Certainly, careful observation of the politics of your office will teach you how *not* to get involved with them, much more effectively than if you were totally ignorant of them. Being clueless just gets you kicked around where you can end up squarely in the middle of the ruckus, sort of akin to an innocent passerby on the steps of the Senate one sunny morning in Rome, looking up at a bird and accidentally stepping right between one of the politicians and old Julius.

Operating Outside the Stream

There are two ways to handle politics: get into the sport of them, or, advertise that you don't play at all.

In this book I'm not going to discuss the science of how to spar with professional gladiators. And perhaps, if that interests you, you may already know how to handle yourself. It is usually the people who find corporate politics distasteful that wind up unarmed in the center of the colosseum. Remember, don't be afraid of politics and don't be disgusted by them or by the people who play the game. Try to stay neutral. As Musashi Miyamoto pointed out, it is the unemotional warrior that has the best chance of living through the battle.

The word we should let resonate here is "compromise." As part of The Three-Fold Path to Mastery you have developed a strong foundation of noble principles to which you aim to adhere throughout your life. Don't compromise them, ever. Don't compromise yourself. Playing politics often requires compromise. Give up turf, give up leverage if you have to, but don't ever give up your insistence to hang onto the principles that form your ideal. Jobs may come and go. You will have to live with yourself for eternity.

Know what your loyalties are and hold fast to them: loyalty to your employer, to your manager and team, and to yourself. Don't be embarrassed by this. Don't allow anyone to make you feel like a loser because you won't play politics, because you won't get involved. As I've mentioned before, your goal is not to be popular or to be cool. It's not to get people to love you or approve of you. Your only goal is to do your work to the best of your ability, to keep your mind in an elevated consciousness, and hopefully, if you are lucky, to actually help others live better and brighter lives.

In the short term as campaigns come and go, you may lose the popularity contest at work. In the long term, particularly if you stick around one company for several years or more, you will find that your colleagues will develop a tremendous respect for you that will go far beyond the shallow appreciation you may have received for playing along with a political game that may have forced you to compromise what you value most.

The Art of War

Read Sun Tzu's *Art of War* – a few times. This set of observations and rules for how to engage in battle was written over two thousand years ago. Some things never change. Business leaders still turn to this book for wisdom and guidance in dealing with corporate, and interpersonal, politics. The book's most valuable lesson can be found in Sun Tzu's definition of the most skillful leaders in battle, as "those who render others' armies helpless without fighting." A good martial artist, he says, "overcomes others' forces without battle, conquers others' cities without siege..."[xxx]

Once you engage, there are always bloody consequences, however few. In battles there is always a winning side and a losing side. Use your skills of perception – that you will improve over time by practicing the techniques in this book – to anticipate potential conflict long before it manifests. Then use your intellect and intuition to evade the conflict when you can.

I grew up in New York and lived there for many years. Though my high school was in a safe neighborhood, one year a few students had gotten mugged within five blocks from the entrance. One of my teachers brought in a former policeman and self-defense expert to give us instruction on how to handle ourselves if we were approached by a mugger. ("Give him whatever he asks for. Don't hesitate. Don't start a confrontation." And so on.) His advice was quite good, but to be honest, my mother's advice was better: "Don't walk down a street if you get a feeling something's not right. Cross the street, go into a nice looking store and wait until you feel safe. Don't be embarrassed about being careful." She must have been a samurai in another life. It was the best advice I ever heard about safety in a big city and I follow it to this day. Just don't be there when it happens. See it coming a mile away. Trust your instincts. Then you don't have to choose how to engage in battle at all. The battle misses you entirely.

This is why in the beginning of the chapter I recommended becoming an expert on the history of your colleagues and the executives of the company. Be *aware* of everything. It's only from your ability to see the maneuvering taking place, that you can anticipate the next moves, and then plan to be far away from the steps of the senate when the crime goes down.

Chapter Summary

Politics & Strategy

- Ignoring corporate politics won't help you and it won't make them go away.
- Read *The Art of War* carefully. Learn the rules. Remember, the most skillful leader is the one who conquers his enemy without fighting.
- Remain loyal to your ideals. Don't compromise yourself for short-lived popularity. Acting with nobility will win you respect over time.
- Stay aware of maneuverings so you can anticipate conflict and evade it entirely.

CHAPTER EXERCISES

POLITICS & STRATEGY

1. *Know Your Opponent*

You may be very friendly with your co-workers. Nevertheless, it is important to understand the motivations of everyone on your playing field. You may never need to engage in politics or corporate combat with others, but you will still need to know what matters to an individual in order to be able to work with him effectively or help him to do his job better. Here are some important facts you may want to discover:

a) How did each person you work with end up in his current job? Your manager? His manager?

b) What are your colleagues' goals? Are they happy doing what they are doing? Are they miserable and looking for a way out? Are they interested in being promoted or are they content with their current position or rank?

c) How does each individual approach problem-solving activities? Some people prefer to take immediate action, using direct confrontation to achieve a resolution. Other people tend to let issues fester before they can get up the courage to talk about solutions. There are many different work and management styles. You don't need to judge them, just understand how each of your colleagues prefers to operate.

d) How does each of your co-workers handle stress and pressure on the job? Some people may become short-tempered, while others can become unusually quiet. Certain individuals can be quite good at hiding the effects of stress. Start to recognize both the obvious and subtle signs when your colleagues are under pressure and you will know when not to push a person too hard. Or, you'll know when to be particularly understanding, and you might make a friend.

KEY #12: WORK ETIQUETTE

"We are here on earth to do good for others. What the others are here for, I don't know."

– W. H. Auden

Have you ever watched movies or read books about the Victorian age, where women are wound up in breath-exterminating corseted dresses and men are turned out in spats and large hats? Everyone addresses each other by their last names even if they are speaking to their own brother or sister. There is bowing and blushing and an abundance of civility. Victorian era society raised the practice of good manners to an art form. In a bestselling book first published in 1879, *A Guide to the Manners, Etiquette, and Deportment of the Most Refined Society*, John H. Young writes:

Nothing is more shameful than a voluntary rudeness. Men have found it necessary as well as agreeable to unite for the common good; they have made laws to restrain the wicked; they have agreed among themselves as to the duties of society, and have annexed an honorable character to the practice of those duties...As culture is the first requirement of good society, so self-improvement should be the aim of each and all of its members. Manners will improve with the cultivation of the mind, until the pleasure and harmony of social intercourse are no longer marred by the introduction of discordant elements, and they only will be excluded from the best society whose lack of education and whose rude manners will totally unfit them for its enjoyments and appreciation...Can anyone fancy what our society might be, if all its members were perfect gentlemen and true ladies, if all the inhabitants of the earth were kind-hearted; if, instead of contending with the faults of our fellows we were each to wage war against our own faults?[xxxi]

Young's observations are still remarkably relevant, despite their historical context. I am happy not to be wearing a corset as I write this book and I wouldn't trade our freedoms or the technological advances achieved in the past century for living in any other age. Nevertheless, there is something to be said for having a bit more corseted-up formality and propriety around the workplace. And as Young points out, cultivating proper etiquette is by nature an activity of self-improvement that ultimately serves the higher purpose of raising the standard of living for everyone.

We can all get awfully sloppy and rude when we are busy. But not expending a certain amount of energy towards proper etiquette at the office is a mistake, if our goal is to encourage productivity, contribute to teamwork and have a decently acceptable quality of life.

Work Etiquette also has a lot to do with ethics. Behaving impeccably at work helps you to avoid the kind of activity that compromises your high principles, and which can get you fired. In this Key I will share with you guidelines to adhere to in order to present the best of yourself to your employer and colleagues, and to distinguish yourself as a knight upholding the most stringent ethical codes of honor.

Experts say most people form a lasting opinion about others within ten seconds of meeting them. Fortunately, good first impressions are as hard to erase as bad ones.

Within your first few days on the job your colleagues and superiors will have solidified their opinions about your work ethic and abilities. Now, you can choose to just follow the rules for Work Etiquette that I will present here and create a regal impression in your coworkers' minds that is the result of no more than superficial mannerisms. However, you will quickly become bored and exhausted if your efforts are merely a charade. It is much easier in the long run and more honest to internalize a strong ethical nature and to practice good etiquette as part of your personal aesthetic, than to try to memorize and adhere to a list of rules regulating your behavior at the office.

When I started working for a financial corporation on Wall Street I was instructed to attend sexual harassment and sensitivity training, required for all new employees. There were a few scenario-based exercises, but ultimately the training was about presenting us with a bunch of rules for how to interact with people of the opposite gender at work. It always struck me as a bit futile, since ethical and sensitive people generally follow reasonable rules anyway. The people who were likely to be the transgressors of insensitive or illegal behavior probably didn't respect social customs to begin with, and – here's the real problem – weren't ethically oriented at the core. It is ethical people who make ethical choices, and sensitive people that behave politely.

So, while you can follow all the guidelines in this Key, and in this book, for making a strong and positive first impression, and for astounding your colleagues with your high-minded behavior, I strenuously recommend striving to become high-minded and ethical and sensitive yourself, rather than simply acting that way between 9 a.m. and 5 p.m.

During the first few weeks of your new job or assignment you will be gathering information about the company, the people you will be working with and the technicalities of the job. Some of the information you may need to gather in order to effectively do your job, as we covered in Key #11, *Politics & Strategy*, may involve hard-to-discover or unofficial information. For example, it is much more likely you will be told what you need to know if you come off as a polite and friendly person, rather than as a rude, self-interested social-climber.

I can't recommend too highly Dale Carnegie's classic manual for interacting with others: *How to Win Friends & Influence People*.[xxxii] Read it several times. Apply the brilliant lessons in this book on how to engage others in conversation, how to make others feel good when they are with you and how to do business with people in the most rewarding way. This book is the foremost guide on etiquette ever written. Do all the things Mr. Carnegie says to do. He knows what he is talking about.

In Key #2, *Acting As If*, we considered the analogy of being a guest in someone's office, as a guide to how to behave. If you have ever worked in a large corporation, where the CEO is never around, then you know how differently everyone acts when they hear he'll be walking the halls one day. They sit up straighter, keep snack bags off their desks, avoid chatting away on personal calls and stay off the internet. I am suggesting that we should act like this every day. This is the evidence of civility that I was referring to in the beginning of this Key. Why should we need the incentive of an executive walking the halls and scrutinizing us like children to behave well at work? Isn't it appropriate, if we are interested in excelling as human beings and cultivating a healthy self-respect, to scrutinize ourselves all the time? Isn't there something a bit dishonest about acting one way when you think no one is looking, and then putting on a show when you think they are?

It may be a challenge to be impeccable all the time. But rather than pretending to be upright as an act of fraudulence once in a while, why not practice *Acting As If* you are upright, with the intention of becoming that some day? Then, when you hear that the CEO is on his way down the hall, you won't have to hurry and sit up straight: you will already be in top form.

Just because you will be cultivating refinement and civility does not mean that you have to be insufferable and boring. With practice, you can allow your natural charisma to flourish, drawing everyone you meet into a circle of warmth, humor and generosity. Don't shut off your inner light in your enthusiasm to be polite. Your ultimate goal is always to contribute to a productive and joyful working environment, for yourself and for others.

Etiquette Guidelines

Now that you understand the foundation of displaying good etiquette at work, here are a few specific guidelines to take you to the next level of comportment:

- Don't curse. Save four-letter words for your private time.
- Don't put your feet up on desks, tables or other chairs.
- Always address people of all levels in a company with the respect you would show a senior executive. Organizational structures often change and you never know who you might end up working for, or needing information from. Take care not to burn bridges or treat anyone with disrespect.

- Don't surf the internet during regular work hours, unless it is specifically your job to do so. I generally caution against surfing the net on break, during lunchtime and after hours as well, since it tends to give others the impression you have too much free time. If you crave a net fix, go to a Kinkos or internet café during your lunch hour and surf with abandon there.

- Walk down hallways quickly and with purpose. If you stroll around, people will think you don't have enough to do. This will irritate people who are busy and stressed out. You need to create the impression that you are aware of how much money it costs your employer for you to get from one end of the hallway to the other. Most employers feel the empty absence of the weight of every penny as it lifts out of their pockets. You don't have to run, mowing down the unsuspecting mail guy and knocking over his cart – just be purposeful in your actions.

- Apply quality control to everything that you do:
  - *Email Etiquette:* Proofread all your memos, documents, e-mail and other written output carefully, no matter how busy you are. Don't be one of those people who sends e-mail that is grammatically challenged, that starts sentences with lowercase letters, or that doesn't include proper punctuation or spelling. It requires more energy from the reader to interpret imperfect messages. When you don't take the time to check your messages, you send the not-so-subtle signal to the reader that they are also not worth much of your time.
  - *Voice Mail Etiquette:* When you leave someone a voice mail message, speak slowly and clearly. Give your phone number at the end of the message, rather than at the beginning, so the person can dial your number or write it down without missing anything you have said. Repeat important information so your colleague doesn't have to replay your message to understand the key points.
  - *Communication Etiquette:* Don't rely exclusively on e-mail to conduct your communications. Sometimes a simple phone call or a short visit to someone's office can be many

times more effective. Any in-person communication is preferable to jotting off an e-mail or leaving a voice message, since standing in front of someone allows the communication to go both ways. Spending the extra few minutes to personalize a conversation will ensure your points are understood and will subtly compliment your colleague by showing him you were willing to take time to see him face to face.

The First Two Weeks

In the beginning of this Key we touched upon the importance of first impressions in a general discussion of etiquette. Here are a few specific guidelines for creating an indelibly positive opinion in your colleagues' minds of your honest and deeply ethical self.

For the first two weeks of a job or assignment be prepared to do extra work and to work longer hours. Although you are naturally a hard worker, you will need to help your colleagues learn this about you right away. Since your goal is to provide your employer with excellent service, strive to create an environment from the start where your co-workers feel good about your ability to provide that service well.

During the first two weeks, try to arrive at the office 15–30 minutes before others in your group normally show up. Then, wait for everyone to leave before heading out. Wait at least 30 minutes. I have found that often a manager will hire you and then get extremely busy the day you start work, fundamentally ignoring you for several days and up to two weeks. This can be an alarming and/or monumentally boring situation to find yourself in. It can also set you up for failure, as your future associates are building their first impressions of you while you are sitting around blowing saliva bubbles at your desk, waiting to be given something to do. Use the extra time you will have in the early morning and late afternoon to get to know your new environment. Walk the halls.

Here are some other suggestions for making the most of your first two weeks:

- Familiarize yourself with the industry the company you now work for is part of, if you are not already familiar with it. Research the company's competitors, target customers, and the direction this industry is taking, according to recent trends and available data from the news and other media sources.

- Locate the company's past three annual reports and read them.
- Browse through the company's intranet and read the bios of the officers – the CEO, COO, CFO/CTO – and other senior executives, to get started on your political investigations.
- Read the company's mission statement.
- Find an organization chart of the corporate officers and org charts of the department you work in and related areas. Identify the names of managers whom you may encounter and what their positions are, relative to the "bigger picture."
- If information about your particular project or colleagues is available, gather it and read it carefully. Memorize as much information as you can about the managers and team members you will be working with. Do non-executive staff have bios posted on the network? Did the company newsletter do a story on anyone you will be working with? Imagine what kind of impression you will make in your first meeting when you can comment on everyone's past projects and successes right after you have been introduced.

Gaining insight into your company and the industry's overall direction, as well as background information on the company's goals, will help you to understand the reasoning behind future company directives, department restructurings and business decisions. Understanding the people behind these decisions, as well as the type of organization they have created or are helping to maintain, will assist you in avoiding political pitfalls, embarrassing yourself in meetings and getting involved in situations you would be better off staying out of.

Keep a Journal

In addition to gathering intelligence by research, make sure you have a method for retaining information you are given during each day, particularly in the early stages of your assignment. I started the practice of keeping a journal for this purpose because my memory would stubbornly refuse to perform even the most basic service when it was presented with too much information at once. I am convinced that people I met on my first work assignments, before I came up with the journal practice, thought I had been dropped on my head as an infant. The journal was a revelation. I would read it over a few times at the end of each day, finally retaining the detailed information. The next day at work I would feel more and more like I belonged there. I would rapidly start to understand the characters and culture. While displaying a good memory of the details of my new environment put my colleagues at ease, it was also infinitely beneficial in acclimating me to my job in a fraction of the time it would have taken otherwise.

Keep your journal stashed in your briefcase or tucked into your suit. When you are introduced to someone or are invited into someone's office for a meeting, make mental notes carefully. As soon as you leave his office, write everything down. Any personal information someone shares with you is obviously important to him. Take care to respect him enough to remember it.

For example, write down details about the project he just completed, a job he once had as a university professor or how his daughter just competed in a piano competition. Write down notes about things you saw in his office that you found intriguing and that might help you engage him in conversation some time in the future. Working with people and getting along with them require being interested in them. Everyone has something unique about him. Find out what that is for each person you encounter and your world at the office will become a great deal more colorful and fun.

The single most important thing you need to remember, of course, is someone's name. Sound easy? In the first day, let alone the first week, of a new assignment, you may be introduced to 20, 30, 40, even 100 new people or more. When you address a colleague by his name after only meeting him once, you will probably fill him with glee. (See Dale Carnegie's book.) Address a colleague by his name right before you ask him how his son did in the play-offs and you'll make a new friend. If you don't address him by name the second time he has given it to you, he will either think you are rude or extremely stupid. Personally, I would try not to take a chance on eliciting either of those first impressions. Remember people's names.

Here are some additional suggestions for practicing proper Work Etiquette that are particularly useful in the beginning of your assignment:

Smile

Smile a lot. Not in a creepy way, like you are auditioning for "The Shining." But smile genuinely and often, when you see a familiar face in the hall, when you pass someone from work outside of the office. Smile at the security guard you see in the morning. When you leave the office late, smile and say goodnight to the cleaning person. If you ever leave something valuable in the office or the bathroom, guess who will be finding it? Smiling at people makes them feel good. It also makes you feel good. It increases your energy and forces you to crawl out of the cave of your chattering mind for a moment and focus on someone else. Studies have proven that the act of smiling actually triggers neurons in your brain that generate feelings of happiness. You don't have to be happy to smile, but you can actually *become* happy by smiling.

Smiling provides a valuable service. The next time you take public transportation or you are on an elevator in an office building, take a good look at the people you are sharing your ride with. Do they look happy? I do this exercise often. What do I see? Too many people who are tired, bored and sad. It reminds me how few people actually enjoy their work and their lives. It's heartbreaking. I know I am lucky to have found work that I love to do, so I try to share some of that good fortune whenever I can by shining a small amount of warmth back into the world. If you are practicing The Three-Fold Path to Mastery, I can almost guarantee you are feeling more contentment and joy in every moment than ninety percent of the people you will encounter during the day. Join me then, in this act of service and kindness, and offer a little bit of your light to others.

Avoid Personal Calls & E-mail

Avoid making personal phone calls and sending personal e-mail from your workplace. Some offices have a policy against this. Many corporations scan e-mail for flags, such as foul language or references to sex, racism and other subjects that could compromise ethics codes. Some companies actually save backups of e-mail traffic for months or even years. You can be fired for even being the recipient of e-mail with questionable content. One solution is to not give out your work e-mail to friends. Discourage colleagues from adding your name to group distribution lists that are used to forward jokes around the office. Don't get caught receiving or sending personal e-mail, or any e-mail, with potentially questionable content. The only certain way to avoid getting caught is to not send or receive these e-mails at all.

Avoid, or limit, personal activity during a paid workday. If you must make a personal call, at least in the first few weeks of your assignment, try to step outside the office and use your cell phone. Once you become more comfortable with your colleagues, you may notice that everyone makes a certain amount of personal phone calls during the day. Use your judgment. Be stricter with yourself than others are. Remember that your purpose is to be the most professional, the most valued, the most productive you possibly can be. You will have to make sacrifices to achieve these goals. Decide what you really want out of your career and then act accordingly.

Be Reserved

Personal information, once it is shared, can't be taken back. How much do your colleagues really need to know about you in order for you to get along with them professionally and for you to do your work well? Every bit of data about your personal life outside the office, past and present, is one more colorful adjective that can potentially distract people from what matters: your expertise and your ability to do your job. Imagine that you are the title of a book. *Your Name,* by You. Every piece of personal information you divulge, perhaps in an effort to make people like you more, is like adding another subtitle to your book title. A few added descriptive words or a phrase, like a subtitle, can be helpful and can make you more approachable and human, just as a subtitle can clarify or enrich the meaning of the book title. However, when you start to fill up the page with modifiers for your title, it has the opposite effect. Each subsequent detail can obscure the meaning of the title or make you forget about it entirely as you process all the new information.

I was working on a Year 2000 project to ensure compliance with the four-digit date code required by computers after the millennium cutover from 1999 to 2000. Towards the end of the project we were working 12 to 14 hour days in order to finish in time. This was one deadline that we could not negotiate. One of the members of the team was a slightly strange chap with significant interpersonal challenges: everyone who knew him disliked him. He was convinced he was superior to everyone else and was happy to let us all know it regularly. One morning, as we were discussing the long hours and how we were all managing to squeeze in enough work each day in order to meet our deadline, our colleague opened up to us and explained his secret: "I can control my bodily functions," he said, "and avoid going to the bathroom for long periods of time." It may seem like a small comment, but you cannot imagine how that little slice of personal detail pushed the envelope of the concept of "need to know." I don't know that anyone present for that exchange has ever forgotten it, or the several seconds of silence that followed his utterance while the rest of us just blinked weakly, wondering what on earth to say to that.

The point is, what you may think is a perfectly reasonable bit of information to share with your colleagues, may be either way too personal for their comfort, or far too defining. Choose carefully what you share with others about yourself. Imagine that someone is taping everything you say about yourself and is composing a bio of you that will be posted in a six-foot high banner above your desk for the rest of your life. If I ever run into the Bathroom Man again, do you think I will have forgotten that comment he made, just because we no longer work for the same company? What you reveal about yourself may define you for a long time. Make sure you apply powerful self-control to your social outings or informal meetings in the cafeteria with colleagues, so that you don't regret your soul-baring later on.

Most people will want to know more about you than you might normally reveal, particularly if you are good at what you do. People see a winner and are interested in how you got that way. Do you have a particular hobby or skill that is unusual and that you spend much of your free time working on? Are you a talented musician or artist? Are you an athlete, a scuba diver or snowboarder? It is acceptable to share information like this, but be general. Don't give away the deepest feelings in your heart about your private journeys in these artistic, creative or athletic areas.

If you have become defined or categorized as a particular kind of person, this limits what you can accomplish for others. It can limit their faith in what you can do, because once you're defined to someone, they box you into their ideas about what someone "like that" can do.

The concept of being reserved about yourself is not intended to increase the focus on your personal life. You will have to use finesse in order to share only what you feel is necessary for you to do your work well. People tend to be curious and may have an interest bordering on obsession to "figure you out." Don't be rude or obtuse. If someone shares a personal detail with you and it feels correct to reciprocate, go ahead. Just choose a detail that is not too revealing or that would compromise your work.

For example, I have always preferred to keep my home address private. My home is my sanctuary, my quiet place to recharge my energy and prepare for my next foray back out into the world. I have not wanted to share with anyone, particularly my work colleagues, where exactly that sanctuary is. For some reason, not wanting to give out a street number, let alone the neighborhood where I live, seems to drive people nuts with curiosity. I finally realized that when I would try to demur answering the "so where do you live?" question – and the one that inevitably follows, "where *exactly?*" – that I was causing feelings of rejection to arise in my questioner. I realized that the other person was hurt that I didn't want him to know this seemingly innocent bit of data about me. That hurt usually turned to anger.

I have had to develop ways of responding to that question and others that will not make anyone else feel bad. For me, out and out lying is not an acceptable solution. Telling an untruth has always made me feel creepy inside. One way I learned to solve the problem was to pick a well-known landmark on the way to my house and ask the person if he is familiar with it. I'll say, "I live just past there." Making my response more personal, but not specific, usually assuages my interrogators. Then, we can both be happy.

Keep in mind that if you give away too much information about your life as a single woman or single man, some people may take this as an invitation to ask you out, despite all the sensitivity training being given these days. Though you may not have intended it, once this switch is on, it is very difficult to turn off without creating a drama you would probably rather not have to deal with at work.

Mundane details of your life that seem to be innocent enough information to share should still only be divulged with care. Professional details such as the industries you have experience with, skills you have mastered, even the university you attended are safe to share. In fact, these details may be common knowledge if your resume was passed around the department before you were hired. Nevertheless, the social details of your life should not be discussed. These kinds of tidbits include: your current romances, vacation details, your financial situation, wild nights partying at the local club, and family disagreements. You are free to make exceptions with close friends that you may meet while working. Again, just use discretion. If you really want to help people and do your best work, remember that divulging personal information at the office usually detracts more from these goals than it contributes.

The ideal work ethic we are trying to cultivate rests just above and beyond what most people think they themselves are capable of. They say that the more exercise you do, the more energy you have – not less. As such, the more you strive for greatness, the more greatness you will exhibit as a human being. It is your willingness to do more, better, with more finesse, more concern, greater attention to detail, greater kindness, better clothes, more follow-through, harder work and better manners that will not only distinguish you professionally – it will make you genuinely happier and more fulfilled by your life.

The principles of *Service, Detachment* and *Humility* as defining characteristics of your life will make you a natural master of Work Etiquette. And a masterfully successful, joyful human being.

CHAPTER SUMMARY

WORK ETIQUETTE

- Improving your Work Etiquette is as important to doing your best work as applying your technical and professional skills to a task is.
- First impressions are powerful and lasting. Use the first two weeks of an assignment to demonstrate to your colleagues what a hardworking, polite person you really are.
- Treat your office as if it is your CEO's home and you are a guest there.
- Be respectful of your good fortune at being employed and make sure every moment of your day is productive, and appears to be productive:
  - Don't surf the Internet or stroll down hallways.
  - Don't send or receive too many personal e-mails and phone calls.
- Display good communication etiquette: Proofread all your documents, e-mail and memos carefully. Speak slowly when you leave a voice message. Try to communicate with others in person whenever possible.
- Learn everything you can about your company, its industry, and the company executives, in order to gain an understanding about current and future business decisions, as well as where your work falls within them.

- Keep a journal with details about everyone you meet and work with in order to assist your memory, and to facilitate your future communications with each person.
- Smile – be friendly. Share your good fortune with others by making them feel good around you.
- Be reserved. Limit the personal information you divulge in order to maintain as professional and undistracting an image as possible.

CHAPTER EXERCISES

WORK ETIQUETTE

1. *Communication Etiquette*

This exercise will help demonstrate the power of a properly composed e-mail and may even convince you to spend the extra minute it might take to send your recipients more formal messages.

a) Open your e-mail application. Start a new message and address it to yourself. In the subject line, type "Chapter?" or leave it blank. In the message area, write this:

> i was wondering can you talk tomorrow about the chapter? call me when you get in -Thx!

b) Send the e-mail and open another new message. Address it to yourself. In the subject line, type "Work Etiquette Exercise 1". In the message area, write this:

> [Your First Name]
> Do you have some free time tomorrow when we can discuss the "Work Etiquette" chapter? Please give me a call with your schedule.
> Thank you,
> [Your First Name]

c) Send the second message and then walk away from your computer. Try to wait an hour or more before you retrieve both the messages you sent.

d) Open the first message marked "Chapter?" How do you feel reading the message? (Try to pretend you didn't write it.) Do you have any immediate impressions about the author? Jot them down on a piece of paper. For example, "Rushed," "Friendly," etc.

e) Open the second message marked "Work Etiquette

Exercise 1". How do you feel reading this message? (Try to pretend you didn't write this one either.) Do you have any immediate impressions about the author? Jot them down on the same piece of paper.
f) Print both messages out. Be objective. How much longer did it take to write the more formal message? How much more professional does it look?

I am not suggesting writing formal e-mails to your close friends if that feels overly stuffy to you; I am just proposing that you take a few extra minutes to compose e-mails that you send as part of your professional life.

2. Perfect For A Day

This exercise is simple: try to follow all of the suggestions in this chapter for Work Etiquette – such as "walking down hallways with purpose," "greeting people by name," "not surfing the internet at the office" and the others – for just one day.

If you can act with perfect etiquette for one hour, let alone a full day, you will have a template for how to work this way all the time. It may seem overwhelming to think about doing all of these things immediately, to attempt a life change overnight. It helps to jump in with both feet and attempt to follow all the suggestions at once for a very limited period of time. Then, incorporate one or two of the suggestions into your daily routine for a few weeks. When you are ready add one or two more. Before long, you will be an impeccable example of professionalism that will win you the respect and admiration of your colleagues, and more importantly, respect for yourself.

Key #13: Deliverables

"If a tree falls in the forest, and there's no one there to hear it, does it make a sound?"
— *classic philosophical question*

One of the simplest, and yet, one of the most career-boosting exercises seems virtually unknown to the vast majority of individuals in the workforce: the activity of producing regular evidence of one's efforts.

We live in a world of capitalist enterprise, based on the principles of commerce. We give something and expect something of equal value in return. We generally expect constant feedback that our transactions have value. Unfortunately, in the professional world our work alone does not always provide tangible proof to our employer that his money was well spent.

In business, the fair exchange of goods and services is a fundamental principle. This is one of the oldest concepts known to man. Whether you are trading products, favors, or using money to represent the value of a transaction, everyone has experienced some kind of commerce. But human beings have a hard time with commercial exchanges that don't place something physical in our hands at the time of purchase. When we buy software, we install it on our computer and use it and we immediately have a tangible thing that delivers a return on our investment. We buy food, and eat it. We buy a movie ticket and we are let into the theater. However, our projects at work move in cycles, and it can sometimes be very difficult to quantify the value of our accomplishments and contributions in the short term.

If you are employed in a leadership role your work may involve tasks like strategic planning, re-engineering, supporting organizational changes or other long-term projects. Some of the business world's hardest workers act as advisors, guides, deputies, shapers and supporters behind the scenes. Often this type of work has value that can't be obviously or easily calculated, or even understood, for months at a time.

How, then, can you reassure your employer and associates that they are getting a fair return on their investment in you? The answer is by producing and communicating Early Wins and Deliverables.

Early Wins

Before your colleagues have a chance to get to know you and respect your work, before you have even had time to grasp your assignment and the environment in which you will be working, your manager is already wondering whether he has made the right decision in hiring you. You will create an atmosphere of great faith in your abilities if you establish and advertise Early Wins.

Early Wins are successes, achieved milestones or other back-pat-inducing accomplishments, which occur towards the beginning of a project, or the start of another phase of a project.

Within a few days of starting your assignment – as soon as possible – deliver some kind of report or document to the person to whom you report. If you can't deliver a plan or schedule for what your activities will be while working on your defined set of tasks, at least deliver your plan for how you will be determining what your activities will be. This will immediately establish a precedent that you are the kind of person who will provide feedback when necessary and get things done.

Your manager will relax and, most importantly, will feel less of a need to watch over you as closely as he might have if you had not set this precedent. You will create confidence in your abilities right away.

The manner in which you communicate your Early Wins, as well as any other achievements or work packages, will probably come in the form of deliverables.

Deliverables

What is a deliverable?

A deliverable is just what it sounds like – something you produce and deliver to someone else. A deliverable can be:

- A document – e.g., describing a project and how its goals will be accomplished
- A status report
- An e-mail message
- A presentation
- A meeting – e.g., a regularly scheduled meeting to discuss project status

Deliverables should be produced throughout the duration of your assignment, not just in the beginning stages as part of showing off Early Wins. You should produce a deliverable whenever there is an opportunity to do so, although in many cases, you will want to limit the time it would take the recipient to review the deliverable. For example, you don't want to be delivering twenty-five page progress reports to a very busy manager who hasn't even asked you to write them. A simple e-mail message may suffice.

To maintain a pattern of delivering tangible evidence of your progress, always deliver a regular, weekly status report of your activities (whether it is requested or not) to the most logical recipient: your direct manager or a senior co-worker, or post the report on a team-focused bulletin board in a common area.

Throughout your work on each assignment, but most importantly in the early stages, look for ways to provide evidence of work accomplished and goals achieved. Set up a string of milestones that can easily be achieved, interspersed with longer-term goals. Identify these milestones to your manager and team, and then remind them when these milestones have been reached by delivering a short report, or an e-mailed note.

Anytime you can mark your work with a deliverable, do it. Towards the end of each defined set of tasks or complete project, start working on an "end of work" report that you can hand over upon the project's conclusion. (We'll address the details of closing down an assignment in Key #16.)

Allow enough time to complete a polished, well-written, proofread document of the work you accomplished. After producing these types of deliverables for several projects I was engaged with early on in my career, a senior manager tracked me down and asked me to give a presentation to his department about the documents. He was thrilled about them and wanted to make the practice standard for everyone in his area.

Creating and highlighting deliverables and Early Wins are also a way for your manager or team to get some easy "bragging rights" about their work. Several teams I worked with developed a newsletter just to communicate activities about our area's projects. We used a software template for newsletters, added some fun graphics and contributed brief blurbs and quotes about our tasks' progress. It became a great conversation piece in meetings and made temporary office celebrities of members of our team, who deserved accolades but whose contributions to the company were often overlooked.

Producing and communicating deliverables and Early Wins is an act of kindness, as much as a personal statement of effort. It can take a great amount of stress off your manager's shoulders, as well as ensure no one takes hard work being done for granted. These simple activities are part of any potential master's toolkit for perfecting the admirable art of service.

CHAPTER SUMMARY

DELIVERABLES

- People are used to getting something tangible in return for money. In fact, people can get upset when they can't "see" what they have paid for.
- Right away, give your employer confidence in you, and in the decision to hire you, by identifying Early Wins: minor – or major – successes that are achieved in the very beginning of your assignment.
- Always provide your manager and/or team members with regular, frequent evidence of your work in the form of deliverables.
- Deliverables can be:
  - Documents
  - E-mail messages
  - Presentations
  - Meetings

CHAPTER EXERCISES

DELIVERABLES

1. *Status Reporting*

Producing a weekly document of your activities and key issues, typically called a Status Report or Activity Report, is an important part of maintaining impeccable business practices. Not all offices have a standard template for these reports, so I have provided an example of the important sections below. A good report highlights major accomplishments as well as issues for review, but remains succinct and well organized so that it can be read and understood quickly.

Activity Report
For Week Ending: [Date]

Tasks Accomplished This Week

- Task description
- Task description

Tasks Planned for Next Week

- Task description
- Task description

Issues

- Issue description
- Issue description

Comments & Questions

The easiest way to complete these reports is to keep updating them throughout the week. On Friday morning, you can edit them into grammatically correct summaries of your work. Regular updates will save you time and energy trying to remember valuable things you may have contributed five days earlier. For this exercise, use the template provided here to fill out a sample Activity Report for your previous week's work *around the house*. This is a fun way to get used to the practice of filling it out. Now you can post your completed report on your home refrigerator and see what happens...On second thought, you can skip that step if you think it might cause more trouble than joy.

KEY #14: FINDING A MENTOR

"The mind is not a vessel to be filled, but a fire to be ignited."
– Plutarch

Finding and engaging the right mentor can be the single most influential career move of your life. Confucius said, "Even when walking in the company of two other men, I am bound to be able to learn from them. The good points of the one I copy; the bad points of the other I correct in myself." With the right attitude you can learn from every person you encounter. In this Key we'll look at how to identify specific people from whom you can gain incomparable wisdom. There are two distinct types of mentors you will identify: the people who know they are your mentors, and the ones who don't.

The word "mentor" derives from the tale in Homer's *Odyssey* which takes place during the Trojan war, when Odysseus entrusts an old man named Mentor with the care of his household and his son Telemachus. Mentor is actually Athena, the Greek goddess of wisdom, in disguise, who provides Telemachus with the guidance and unique teaching that only an immortal deity could. During Telemachus' own journeys years later, the advice the wise Mentor had given him saved his life many times.[xxxiii]

The concept of a wise and experienced teacher helping a younger adept mature has remained an appealing and beloved way of passing the torch between generations, though mentoring does not necessarily require any age difference at all. A mentor is, historically, a person who has achieved a certain amount of professional recognition or expertise in a particular field, who then assists someone else in achieving goals in the same, or a related, field.

Mentors can be invaluable in providing privileged information about how to get ahead for those new to an industry or organization. Mentors can open up doors for their apprentices through their many contacts as well.

However, a mentor can also be from an entirely different professional background and still be able to provide valuable support and information. For example, some women have found that professional advice on becoming successful in business can be just as insightful coming from a music industry CEO, as from a Wall Street CEO – if the CEO is a woman. Her advice, in that case, may be more gender-specific than industry-specific, but no less illuminating.

A mentor can be a guide, a hero, a confidante, a teacher. Some people become very close to their mentors, forming life-long friendships. Others remain distant, but still find the relationship extremely beneficial in developing their careers.

There's a great humility – and wisdom – in seeking out mentors throughout your life. You may even be fortunate enough to encounter a mentor with a capital "M" who will be the golden thread that weaves into your world and your consciousness and becomes an elemental part of your personal and professional evolution.

The Official Mentor

There is a traditional practice in certain Buddhist religions of recognizing and finding *tulkus*, reincarnated masters, when they are still young children, taking them from their homes and instating them in a monastery for training. Families within these cultures consider it a great honor to have their child recognized by senior monks and removed to the temple, and it is believed to confer upon several generations blessings of protection and liberation from suffering. After passing a variety of tests designed to prove the child is the true reincarnation of the monks' teacher, the child is then revered as the living master. The child is assigned one or a few special tutors who provide him with a comprehensive and broad education in many subjects, including secrets of the spiritual lineage, which few disciples would ever be privileged to hear. He is eventually presented with the keys to the kingdom, often quite literally. The treasures of the monastery are in his hands, though as a monk, he would never actually "own" them himself.

The idea of being recognized as "the chosen one" may sound appealing; and being trained to take over the kingdom even more attractive. It is not impossible to experience the equivalent of this in the professional world. However, the odds are that you will have to be the one to seek out your teachers with enthusiasm and persistence, as opposed to the likelihood that they will come hunting for you. Certainly if you are interested in possessing the treasures of the kingdom, you will probably be more successful in finding them with the help of those who know exactly what they are and where to find them. In the business world the treasures we seek are not always material. As in a monk's spiritual training, these treasures are jewels of wisdom cloaked in the fog of ignorance that only a mentor – or a lifetime of experience – can reveal.

Your official, or primary, mentor is most likely to be a person with whom you directly discuss your career; in other words, a person who knows he is acting as your mentor.

Choose your primary mentor carefully. You will probably find that one mentor in particular, if selected and treated with care, will remain influential in your life for a long time.

If you are not sure whom you should approach to be your mentor, consider that you may not yet have found the right person. Be patient. Following are a few suggestions for identifying your mentor.

Do Research

If you prefer not to wait to accidentally cross paths with your potential mentor and want to proactively locate someone immediately, do research. Consult trade publications or probe the internet for information about successful executives or super-achievers in your field. Some of the most accomplished people in an industry eventually go on to do other things with their careers, such as becoming authors, speakers and/or consultants. This makes them easier to find, but harder to communicate with. Don't limit your interest to quasi-celebrities. The quiet millionaire living around the block might have much more valuable insight to offer, and may also have more free time to spend helping you.

Attend Meetings

Another way to find a mentor is to attend professional gatherings within your industry. For example, attend banking, insurance, publishing, legal, medical or other trade shows and conferences. Join a professional organization. Professional organizations exist for every major industry and a wide variety of special interests; they also usually have regional chapters offering meetings, presentations, networking opportunities and even training and certification in niche subjects. The internet provides a vast source of information about these types of organizations. Search under "professional organizations" in your web browser for an extensive listing.

Some of these organizations also have formal mentoring programs that you can participate in. These programs have already identified successful people who are interested in acting as mentors and they will match you up with a qualified expert. While these programs can be useful, it is nevertheless uniquely powerful to identify a mentor on your own. This is an individual whom you truly admire, and who you just know would inspire you to greatness if you had a chance to meet and speak with him.

For the patient, persuasive and brave among you, there is always the possibility of finding a "celebrity" mentor. These individuals are stars in their respective industries, if not in Hollywood. Though these people seem impossibly busy and important, they do occasionally respond to the well-written, well-timed letter or e-mail. Even famous people get a kick out of helping someone else become successful. Don't go after a mentor just because he or she is a celebrity. However, if you find that you deeply respect a famous person, and you feel that speaking with this person would fill you with wisdom and enthusiasm for your work, then make a commitment to pursue this person's advice with determination – and an excess of tact.

Convincing The Chosen One to Mentor You

Once you have identified your ideal mentor, what is the appropriate way to approach this person?

There is a revered, and some say mythical, saint named Babaji, who has lived in the high Himalayas for centuries. It is said that he is impossible to find, though spiritual seekers from India and elsewhere have tried, often perishing on the quest in the freezing and unforgiving regions where the legends of Babaji place him. Stories describe him as the master of all teachers, a magnificent and holy being who can not only teleport himself from one place to another, but who can bring his entire circle of disciples with him. One might imagine if he were to choose to, he could simply dissolve his form when he sensed a less than sincere student approaching and reappear elsewhere. (And don't we all wish we had that skill at times!) There was, however, a very sincere seeker who was desperate to find Babaji and beg him to be his teacher. He sought Babaji throughout most of his life, going on pilgrimages in the mountains of the Himalayas, praying and meditating on where the elusive teacher might be. It was said that a pure individual could see Babaji as a bright point of light hovering on top of a mountain. His students would appear as a ring of bright lights around him.

One night, our desperate seeker was praying and walking around the base of a mountain when he saw the ring of lights and then the single bright light in the center. Overcome with joy, tears streaming down his face, he spent the next two days hiking to the top of the mountain. When finally he reached the top, sure enough, there was the great saint, hair flowing in the wind, talking to his students. The seeker ran over to Babaji, threw himself at the master's feet and choked out his story. "I have been looking for you for over 40 years!" he cried, "Now that I have finally found you, after all my hardship, please you must take me as your disciple."

Babaji said, "No." And went back to teaching his students.

The seeker was undeterred. It was common for spiritual teachers to refuse this kind of request several times before acquiescing. Nevertheless, though he asked three more times, "Be my teacher!" Babaji said, "No." Finally, after his years of searching, of holding in his heart Babaji's acceptance of him as his only reason for living, he declared, "Master, if you will not teach me, I will throw myself off the mountain to my death." He meant it. Utterly.

Babaji looked over at him and, actually appearing to be bored, said, "Fine. Do it."

Without a millisecond of hesitation, the seeker ran to the edge of the mountaintop and jumped to his death. Moments later the students heard his body crash against the rocks. They raced over to the edge of the cliff and looked down at the body. The seeker was dead. Babaji sighed and said, "Well, I guess you had better go get him." The students carried the seeker's lifeless body back to the mountaintop where Babaji was waiting for them. The saint knelt down over the seeker, closed his eyes, touched the seeker's forehead, and brought him back to life.

"Go sit in the circle," Babaji said to him.

Later, the saint asked his students if they knew why he had brought the student back to life and agreed to be his teacher. They answered, "Because he was willing to jump off the mountain to his death if you wouldn't."

"No," Babaji said, "Because when I told him to go ahead and do it, that was a test of how he would respect my teaching. I was not impressed that he jumped. It was that he did it without any hesitation."[xxxiv]

Why did I tell you that story? It wasn't just because it is beautiful. It is an illustration of the proper way to respect the teacher or mentor relationship once you have the great fortune of being part of one. Choose your mentor carefully. Once you have and once he has accepted the responsibility of working with you, do the things he suggests without hesitation. If you don't trust someone enough to follow his suggestions, don't waste your time apprenticing yourself to him. Suggestions you may be given may not always seem logical. For example, my first mentor told me to do product sales for a few months. To say that at the time I loathed the idea of, let alone the reality of sales, would be an understatement. I was shy and soft-spoken, a writer for goodness' sake! How could I sell anything at all? Nevertheless, I trusted my mentor completely. He knew what I wanted to know, and he had what I wanted to have. I took a job giving sales presentations on behalf of a software company days after his suggestion. The time I spent traveling around the country doing sales was one of the most transformational and influential periods of my life, let alone my career. I never, never would have thought to do something like that on my own, and I would not have taken the suggestion seriously if it had not come from someone I trusted so implicitly. So, choose your mentor very carefully, and once you have, be humble enough to respect and honor his advice.

Now, let's look at how a modern businessperson might request a mentor's help, since performing full prostrations on a man's carpet could be misinterpreted and most women executives will prefer you not slobber over their $500 Manolo Blahniks, thank you very much.

So, how do you convince your ideal mentor to work with you? Well, how do you make a friend?

A friend is made by discovering a foundation of common interests, beliefs or other powerful character traits. A good friend is made little by little, by gently giving the other person "gifts" of your faith and respect, until you both realize that you trust each other.

How does making a good friend relate to "making" a mentor? Getting a mentor is not a simple transaction. You don't hand over a check for $1000 and then sit in the mentor's office for exactly one hour while he spouts pearls of wisdom in your direction. A mentor works, generally, for free. Like a friend, your mentor will take a personal interest in your career path, giving you suggestions on everything from what books to read to what kind of suits to buy. Your mentor will answer your calls (within a reasonable timeframe) and talk you through difficult decisions and anxious moments.

Why would an important person spend his precious time and energy, freely giving away the secrets it took him an entire career to discover? Because people like to give back. Believe it or not, despite the competitiveness and fierceness of the business world, there are plenty of people who are grateful for an opportunity to help another person become successful. Once you have reached the top of your career, you may find it equally rewarding to share what you have learned with others. That is why so many top executives and other stars in their fields start giving presentations, writing and teaching, once they have taken their careers as far as they will go, or have retired from a lifetime of successes. One of the most natural human instincts is to teach what you know once you know something worth teaching.

Nevertheless, why should your chosen mentor, mentor *you*? That is the question you must answer for them as you begin to build a relationship. Your ability to show your chosen mentor why you are deserving of their time, will determine how much of their time you are allotted.

The Initial Contact

Carefully plan your first contact with your mentor. How will you approach this person? By letter? E-mail? In person, following a presentation or a guest appearance?

Dale Carnegie's *How to Win Friends & Influence People,* the book we considered in Key #12, *Work Etiquette,* also offers excellent advice on how to construct a letter of introduction to someone special, so that you are most likely to gain a response. Carnegie points out that nearly every individual is moved by other people taking a personal interest in him.[xxxv] Find out everything you can about a potential mentor before approaching him. In your initial contact, be specific about what he has accomplished in his career that interests you. Let him know how serious you are about becoming successful and assure him that you would treat any advice he could give you with the greatest respect.

Be persistent. Don't be a stalker, just persistent. For example, if you don't get a response to your first letter after a few weeks, send a second letter describing yourself in more detail, and perhaps, asking the person a specific question. Enclose an SASE inside your letters, with your contact information – including phone, e-mail and address. If you have no response after a third communication, look for another mentor. Don't assume your first choice is a "bad" person, or any other negative adjective you may be tempted to use after your rejection. Some people really are extremely busy and others don't even read mail from return addressees they don't recognize. Just find someone else who inspires you. There must be more than one.

Always remember to be grateful to the person who has guided you, however trivial the advice. Gratitude goes a long way toward maintaining relationships. The best way to thank a mentor is to follow his advice and actually become successful yourself. In fact, your eventual success may turn out to be more rewarding to your mentor than his own achievements.

Though you may only find one special mentor to guide you along your career path, you can utilize countless other professionals as mentors, whether they know they are mentoring you or not.

The Unofficial Mentor

Few people can be called true masters, in the comprehensive Three-Fold Path sense. However, lots of people are masters in a specific area. While you may never encounter or see a legendary "saint" of business, you will likely encounter numerous professionals who are absolutely flawless in an area in which you are seeking improvement.

For example, you may be waiting for a meeting to start when suddenly, a manager enters the room whose very presence is so dynamic and powerful that everyone quiets down until the person reaches a chair and gets settled. Be aware of people like this. Observe them carefully. What is it about them that causes others to react with respect, awe, or deference in their presence?

Study successful people. Reflect on their achievements, their inner as well as their more obvious choices. What do they wear? How do they carry themselves? How do they talk to low-ranking staff members when it appears no one is around to hear them? How do they shake hands and introduce themselves? How do they sit? How do they inspire people – or perhaps how do they frighten people?

Any person whom you have decided to observe, who has influenced your actions or choices, is your mentor. Have lots of unofficial mentors. Keep your eyes open for intriguing characters. Someone always does something better than you do. Always be ready to learn something new, adopt a new behavior or way of acting, to improve your game, and to evolve yourself.

You may even send someone a letter after you have used him as an unofficial mentor, thanking him for showing you how to do something better. You never know where that might take you.

Finally, when a young, inexperienced businessperson sends you a letter asking if you will answer a couple of questions, because your career has really, really inspired him…be as humble, as kind, and as forthcoming with him as you hope your next mentor will be with you.

CHAPTER SUMMARY

FINDING A MENTOR

- A mentor is a person who has achieved professional recognition or expertise in a particular field, who then assists someone else in achieving goals in the same or a related field.
- Getting a mentor is like making a friend: it takes respect, trust, common interests and patience.
- Choose your mentors carefully: find them by doing research and attending professional meetings. Once you have a mentor, trust his guidance.
- You can have countless "unofficial" mentors just by being observant.
- Always be thankful for and gracious about your mentor's guidance, whether officially or unofficially given. Show your gratitude by writing a note of thanks, or by simply becoming successful through your mentor's advice.

CHAPTER EXERCISES

FINDING A MENTOR

1. *Identifying Your Top Ten*

a) Off the top of your head list the names of as many people in your industry as you can, up to ten, who you believe would make excellent mentors.

b) Now do some research. For example, read professional trade magazines and browse relevant websites. Find out the names of the most accomplished people in your industry. Most of us can't name many Nobel prize winners, but we can easily tell you who starred in the latest Hollywood blockbuster; the point being that you may have a wealth of undiscovered treasures in your industry who may be more attentive to your questions than the obvious choices you may have made before researching all your options.

c) After a few weeks of research, make another Top Ten list. You may find that your new list has different names on it than your first list.

d) Narrow your list down to three names. What are your common interests? What motivates you and inspires you the most about each of these three potential mentors?

e) In one, grammatically perfect, compelling sentence, describe why each of your top three choices should be your mentor.

You may decide not to contact anyone about becoming your mentor, and you may instead decide to rely on having many "unofficial" mentors. Nevertheless, the above exercise can still be useful. Consider this: what made each person on your final list so accomplished? Now you have a better sense of the goals most important to you as you evolve in this field.

KEY #15: WARRIOR TRAINING

"This is my body. And I can do whatever I want to it. I can push it. Study it. Tweak it. Listen to it. Everybody wants to know what I'm on. What am I on? I'm on my bike busting my ass six hours a day. What are you on?"

– Lance Armstrong

There are secret techniques mastered by the world's most successful people, including CEOs, Olympic athletes, entrepreneurs, yoga masters, billionaires, great artists and monks; techniques that are simple in concept, yet unimaginably potent.

In this Key you will learn how the methods of the Warrior are part of the art of mastering yourself – not engaging in conflict with others, as one might incorrectly assume. Warrior Training describes the non-violent secrets for reaching extraordinary heights of achievement and happiness, based on different ways to monitor and modify mental and physical activity throughout each day. Your self-mastery will become a reality through a continuous effort to elevate, conserve and store your energy. Gaining control over your body, mind and spirit, you will learn how to utilize your stored energy, turning it into inconceivable personal power.

The warrior attitude is best described in this poetic writing by the Thirteenth Dalai Lama, from his *Discourse on the Great 'Lam Rim'*:

The Bodhisattva is like the mightiest of warriors; but his enemies are not common foes of flesh and bone. His fight is with the inner delusions, the afflictions of self-cherishing and ego-grasping; those most terrible of demons that catch

*living beings in the snare of confusion and cause them for-
ever to wander in pain, frustration and sorrow. His mission
is to harm ignorance and delusion, never living beings.
These he looks upon with kindness, patience and empathy,
cherishing them like a mother cherishes her only child. He
is the real hero, calmly facing any hardship in order to
bring peace, happiness and liberation to the world.*[xxxvi]

I heard a story a few years ago about a young, but spiritually
advanced Buddhist monk, who was walking home from a lecture
one night in Connecticut. He was not Asian and he always dressed
in western clothes. Despite his contemplative demeanor and his ability to enter the exalted inner state of *samadhi* when he meditated,
few people could have recognized him as a monk. He was alone and
it had just rained that afternoon. The pavement was shiny under the
glow of the streetlamps. The monk heard the sound of a foot splash-
ing into a puddle just before a man stepped out in front of him holding a knife. The man was small and his clothes were dirty. He
appeared to have been living on the streets, though his eyes were not
yet hardened. The monk said later that the man looked frightened,
as if this were the first time he had ever tried to mug anyone. "I have
a knife," the man said, stepping towards him. The monk was calm.
From years of meditation, the monk had become very sensitive to
others' thoughts. He could see clearly now that the man was unsure
whether he wanted to be mugging someone.

The monk reached into his pocket and replied, "I have something even more powerful than a knife." The man stopped moving
and looked at him, childlike. The monk pulled out his wallet and,
under a shaft of light from the streetlamp, held up a crisp one hundred dollar bill. The mugger dropped to his knees on the wet pavement, the knife loose in his hand. He began to sob. The monk gave
the man all of the money left in his wallet and walked away.

The complicated and profound teaching the young monk gave
his attacker that evening never fails to move me and to cause me
to reflect. Though the monk held up the hundred-dollar bill as
something more powerful than a knife, I think the story really
demonstrates the power of a strong mind. The monk used his intuition and his fearlessness not only to save himself, but to save
another person – the very person that was threatening to harm

him. I've spoken to many people who have heard this story. We all came to the same conclusion: that the man would never attempt to mug anyone again. I like to imagine that he found peace somehow, and perhaps is healthy and earning money more conventionally as a result of the monk's unusual lesson and compassionate blessing.

The circumstances of this story could have turned out differently. If the monk had less self-control, he might have lost precious energy reacting to the situation with extreme fear or anger. Instead, both he and his attacker emerged unharmed, and one might even say they were both transformed by the experience. Thus, a situation that could have destroyed one or both of them, in fact, made them both stronger.

As this story demonstrates, Warrior Training can teach us to react to conflict in uncommon ways. Calm and deliberate, we are able to rise to any challenge. And regardless of our own circumstances, we are able to use any situation to offer knowledge or kindness to others.

Warrior Training is the preparation for attaining mastery. The training includes learning and practicing techniques for overcoming our lower nature, which takes away our clarity and weakens our self-control. Warriors engage in a ceaseless combat against selfishness and laziness. The battle is won when we have reached a profound and immutable joy regardless of our circumstances. Until then, we keep fighting, day by day, minute by minute. One day we realize that the struggle itself is thrilling. And we come to understand that we are not just fighting for our own self-improvement, but for the courage, the strength and the mental acuity to help others become warriors themselves.

Every person who has figured out how to perform an activity exceptionally well has attained some level of skill in the warrior arts, whether he is aware of this or not. Every star athlete, every best-selling writer, every corporate CEO, every master consultant is a warrior of some kind.

At any precise moment in time, you are either gaining energy or losing energy. There is no resting state. Masters know this and, therefore, monitor their mental and physical activity carefully to ensure that they are gaining energy throughout each day, rather than losing energy.

Following The Three-Fold Path to Mastery is demanding. The discipline right work requires is enormous. Only those in peak physical and mental condition will have enough energy to succeed. A person with the ability to keep his energy level high is capable of achieving more than the average person, who has less energy with which to accomplish desired tasks. As you maintain high energy levels, your body of consciousness, which we can call the "subtle body," can actually store unused energy for use in times of increased stress or great challenge. The subtle body is the energetic body of consciousness that directs higher spiritual thought and intent. The subtle body is made entirely of vibrations of energy appearing as light and can be felt physically and seen by the eyes with practice. Stored energy in the subtle body is what creates personal power.

You can always recognize someone with above average personal power. These are the people who seem to buzz with electricity when they enter a room. These are people who may be unusually charismatic, bright, intelligent, insightful. These people seem to accomplish much more than the average human being – working a full day, exercising, taking professional classes, maintaining a couple of hobbies on the side, volunteering for charities, and keeping a perfectly decorated and clean home. Or, people with great personal power may simply seem uniquely peaceful and wise. These are people who may not speak often, but speak precisely. They appear to have an inner radiance and seem somewhat unfazed by external events.

Personal power is a quality that everyone cherishes. We admire those who have it. For those with personal power, life always seems to go their way. Why is that? Is life really always going their way, or are these people deeply content in a way that allows them to remain centered regardless of what happens to them? Being able to remain at peace despite the circumstances of your life requires personal power.

Rather than remaining an idle and complacent observer, a warrior takes control of his circumstances and, using simple techniques, generates the power necessary to architect his life as he chooses.

Being a warrior simply means accepting responsibility for your life. The way to achieve this is to cultivate a strong body, a strong mind, and a strong spirit.

Strong Body

Having physical stamina is necessary in order to increase your personal power. Your body is a living organism, which hosts your mind and your spirit. In order to maximize your mental agility you will need to improve your overall health. You do this with exercise.

Exercise is a powerful way to clear the mind of clutter. The time you spend exercising is free time away from your routines, where you allow your mind to rest and your blood to pump oxygen into your brain. After a vigorous workout, you will always be more relaxed and able to think more clearly.

Physical stamina makes it easier to get through a day of work. Commuting to and from work you may run for the train, race after a taxi, and hike up a flight or two of stairs. During the day you may fly down hallways to get to a meeting on time, going from one office to the next for hours without a break. You may get stuck in a meeting that lasts over an hour with the lights dimmed and a mind-bogglingly dull slide show clicking by one slow frame at a time. You may have to bathe small children, teach a full day of classes to teenagers, or bus dirty tables until four in the morning. All of these moments are made less draining if you exercise regularly, if you have physical stamina.

Finally, when challenging situations present themselves, if you work out and your body is strong, you will simply have more inner strength to face these situations. You will feel powerful in your limbs and your lungs, and therefore, you will be more equipped to stand up to tumult than if you felt weak. Physical stamina gives you the body of a warrior, rather than that of a victim.

While all forms of exercise are beneficial, certainly any form of exercise that is interesting enough to get you to keep doing it, some forms of exercise are particularly good for increasing your personal power as well as your stamina.

These forms of exercise are martial arts; yoga; and running, hiking, or walking. (Remember, it's important to be sensitive to your body and conditioning – check with your physician before beginning any new or challenging physical activity.)

Martial Arts

Martial arts include karate, tae kwon do, aikido, kung fu, jujitsu, tai chi, and many others. It is believed that some of these ancient arts were first developed by Bodhidharma, a venerated Buddhist teacher, who realized that monks living in monasteries in China were spending hours strengthening their minds in meditation, but neglecting their bodies. Bodhidharma created a series of exercises, like a moving meditation, in order to help the monks balance the strength of their minds with equally strong physical conditioning. Different forms of these original exercises later emerged in countries across the world, including Japan, Korea, and eventually, the United States. Most of the martial arts have at their foundation some methodology for increasing personal energy and even becoming enlightened. Excelling in the martial arts involves continuous study.

Constantly learning new techniques keeps your workout fresh and your mind sharp. As you progress in one of these arts, you will begin to see an improvement in your ability to deflect conflict and handle antagonistic people. You will see an increase in your personal power, as you realize how much physical strength you are gaining. Nevertheless, you will become less likely to engage in conflict once you realize the potential futility of it, and you will hesitate to use force once you have learned the destructive power of a single technique.

In particular, martial arts cannot be too highly recommended for women. Feeling physically formidable can help you stand up in front of a roomful of men, who may be higher-ranking, older or just skeptical of your abilities, and not hesitate to give the finest presentation of your career. Women are often socialized to be quiet, polite, accommodating, and worst of all, insecure about their abilities. Martial arts training can help to erase all of that brainwashing and allow you to play on the same field as all of your colleagues – male or female. The physical power and disciplined training will give anyone confidence, but it is often women who so badly need it.

In the early 1990s I was invited to speak to a U.S. Air Force technology group at the Pentagon, and to provide a motivational and instructional talk on using software to benchmark projects.

Though a colleague of mine would be attending with me, I would be speaking alone.

In order to be let into the Pentagon on the day of the meeting, we had to provide a contact with our birthdates and social security numbers in advance for a background check. After being escorted down long, uncarpeted corridors that seemed unchanged since the fifties, we arrived at the conference room where I would be speaking. There were two marines flanking the door of the room in full dress uniforms, including white gloves and rifles. Large letters mounted on the side of the wall to the left of the entrance spelled out, "Top Secret." I wondered how on earth I had wandered into this situation. I was too young, too inexperienced to be doing this. Fear began to spread rapidly through my nervous system, threatening to shut off my motor skills entirely.

I set up my laptop in front of the room, connected it to the projection equipment and watched the slideshow I had prepared pop up onto the large screen. Then, I tried valiantly to look perfectly normal while I watched thirty men in uniform file into the room and take their seats. One or two civilians showed up and one, pretty Asian woman.

If someone asked me to come up with a more intimidating scenario than this one, I'm not sure I could have succeeded. People had run out of chairs and were standing up in the corner, blocking the door. Clearly, at this point, there was no chance of escape. So I pictured myself in the strongest personal moment I could remember: at the dojo, in my karate uniform, doing roundhouse kicks against a pad. Though I did not go through the military's training, as rigorous as I imagined that was, I knew I had taken my physical and mental stamina at least to the level of the people in the room, just through a different pathway. Reminding myself how hard I had trained in the dojo filled me with an unusual energy and confidence. "You know project management," I told myself, "You have something worthy to share here." I made it through the presentation and I remember hearing applause. What was important, and what I have never forgotten, was how the practice of martial arts helped me to erase a lifetime of conditioning and a moment of overwhelming insecurity. It helped me to get a job done that I was capable of doing, despite my fear. Now, I recommend martial arts to everyone who asks me how to overcome personal challenges, and particularly for women.

For those people who would prefer a gentler martial art, I recommend tai chi. Tai chi is excellent for raising your energy level and developing physical stamina at a more moderate pace. With enough practice all the martial arts, including the styles that appear gentler, can help the disciplined student develop a high degree of power and energy.

Yoga

There are many different kinds of yoga, but all of the varieties share the basic practices of breathing combined with strategic body positions and stretches. (The word "yoga", meaning "union" in Sanskrit, is also used to refer to the esoteric practices, involving the mind and the heart, for attaining union with God. Here, I am referring specifically to the practices of physical yoga often called *Hatha Yoga,* which in Sanskrit means "union of force.")

Yoga, if practiced over time, will provide powerful conditioning as well as teach techniques for relaxing the body and mind. Many forms of yoga can be as physically strenuous as any other form of exercise.

Practicing yoga is extremely helpful as part of a program for increasing energy. Energy moves throughout the body via a fascinating and intricate set of subtle channels or highways, called *nadis* or streams. The most powerful channel is called the *shushumna,* which runs parallel to the spine and directs flowing energy from a point at the base of the vertebrae through centers of energy called "chakras" up to the third eye (a point approximately one inch above the center of the eyebrows). In advanced yogis the energy can continue to flow past the third eye and up through the crown chakra, located above the top of the head; at this time an individual enters the extremely blissful inner state called *samadhi.*

When the chakras, aligned along the *shushumna,* are open and pure, energy can move freely through the body. This provides an individual with virtually unlimited vitality, health and inner peace. However, for most people these energy centers can be clogged with obstructions, resulting from a variety of issues such as unresolved emotional conflict or physical injury, preventing our source of vitality from flowing freely. Blocked energy can be responsible for a number of different physical ailments, and can also be responsible for fatigue and feelings of laziness, sadness and lethargy. Among other practices including introspection and meditation, yoga will help release blocked energy, providing you with feelings of exhilaration and lightness both during and after exercise sessions.

Running/Walking/Hiking

Running and hiking are particularly powerful ways to improve cardiovascular health and physical stamina, while also allowing you some time alone. Running and hiking are easy. You don't need a teacher. You don't need to adhere to a class schedule or cram into a room filled with other stressed out people in order to get your exercise. You don't need cumbersome or expensive equipment. All you need are proper shoes and motivation. Walking is a noble substitute for hiking or running, if you are injured, have weak knees, or for any other reason you are not physically able to hike or run. All of these activities will also enable you to exercise outdoors – when possible in clear, clean, natural settings with trees and pretty scenery.

Strong Mind

A strong mind is the ultimate defense against a dull, meaningless life. With a strong mind, you can always think yourself into better circumstances. As Buddha said, "You are what you think. Everything you are arises with your thoughts. With your thoughts you make the world."[xxxvii] Mental fortitude gives you the power to see for yourself better ways of doing things, better choices to make, better ways of handling difficult situations.

Increasing the agility of your mind will make you more productive, more efficient, and obviously, smarter. Like any muscle, the mind atrophies without use. The mind needs stimulation. The best way to stimulate the mind is to constantly feed it new information, force it to learn, expand, change.

Continuous Learning

Sir Francis Bacon said, "Knowledge and human power are synonymous." Every day is an opportunity to learn something new, to open your mind to new possibilities, and to ignite new fires of passion for subjects you might never have imagined were interesting. One should approach every moment of the day with Beginner's Mind (as described in Key #6, *Impermanence*), considering all of life as one's teacher. It is also powerful to take what you might learn into your own hands and sign up for a class. Options for continuing your education abound. You can sign up for an adult education class at a local university in a topic that interests you, even if it has nothing to do with your career. You can even make the commitment to study for a graduate degree. Applying the level of discipline required in order to attain a masters or doctorate degree can change you completely. The point is to never stop feeding your imagination or stop opening your spirit to new possibilities.

Read Books

Balance the "easy reads" with literary or nonfiction books that are more complex and educational, that stretch your vocabulary and encourage contemplation and reflection.

Learn Computer Science

Anyone in the business world seeking the highest levels of management and compensation would do well to know some aspect of current computer technology intimately. Computers will only become more influential in our lives over time, not less. Even if your work is not based in a corporate office environment, such as work in the medical and healing professions, the art world or teaching, computers will always play a role. You will be much more valuable to employers if you understand the technology that drives or supports the majority of business decisions these days.

A side benefit (or primary one, depending on your perspective) is that learning computer science can actually strengthen your mind. Programming a computer, or understanding the complexities of networking computers and telecommunications equipment, is a modern version of ancient mental exercises.

As introduced earlier in this book, for centuries Buddhist monks have spent hours every day, developing their minds by gazing at and eventually memorizing intricate geometric pictures called *mandalas*. Some of these exquisite paintings resemble the optical effect of seeing an image in a mirror facing another mirror: the image appears to repeat itself within itself into infinity. The monks' objective is to be able to hold in their minds an entire *mandala*, with all of its miniscule detail and colorful ornamentation. This helps them to meditate better. They practice this mind-strengthening exercise for hours upon hours, day after day.

The structures you need to hold in your mind, in order to successfully solve a business problem through computer code, are surprisingly similar to the ancient practice of memorizing and visualizing *mandalas*. Why not strengthen your mind, and get paid for it?

Interestingly, musicians experience the same kind of mind-stretching through their work as programmers do through designing and writing computer code or systems. Many computer technologists have musical backgrounds, and musicians tend to make successful computer programmers.

Job applicants with strong backgrounds in computer technology have a much richer field to plow when looking for work. The influence of computer technology in every walk of life grows by leaps each year, and companies are always hungry for resources who are proficient in the latest technologies.

For a boost in mental strength as well as paycheck size, computer science is a smart field to pursue professionally, and an excellent educational direction for evolving your mind.

Limit TV

In addition to keeping your energy high through education and reading, you can ensure your energy doesn't drop by not turning on the television. Imagine all the people out there, who work a typical 9-to-5 day, then come home and flip on the television. If your goal is to be typical, then go ahead and watch lots of TV. If your goal is to attain mastery, to be the most intelligent, most productive, most noble, and most highly paid of all workers, you cannot do the same things that typical people do. You have to do things that typical people don't do, or won't do, because they don't have the desire or the discipline. TV networks you into the minds of all the ordinary people in the world. If you want your mind to be sharper than ordinary minds, if you want an edge, here is the secret: watch TV moderately.

Watching TV is one activity where there is no question you are losing energy. There is no interaction. No mental exercise. You are watching others having a life, rather than having one. Studies have shown that the mind is more active *while you are sleeping,* than while you are watching television.

Watching the occasional video is different. A video is not networked. You are not online mentally to millions of other people at the very same time. You are home, alone or with a few others, watching a story unfold in a focused, commercial-free, offline manner. Select the kinds of movies to watch on video which will inspire you, make you laugh, get your heart rate going. If a movie you've rented is dull, or for some reason, is not making you feel good, shut it off. Time is precious. Isn't an hour of your time worth more than the few dollars you paid to rent an awful movie?

Even videos shouldn't become your primary leisure activity. All passive activity should be enjoyed in moderation. An accurate gauge for the power of any activity to energize you should be how you feel afterwards. After you watch a lot of TV, or even too many videos or movies, you often feel tired, lethargic. Instead, take a walk in nature – in a safe park, or along a beach – read a book, write in a journal. These activities tend to make you feel energized afterwards. Monitor yourself and make the decisions about what to spend your precious leisure time pursuing based on the level of energy you want to have in your life.

Strong Spirit

With a strong spirit, a strong mind and strong body will naturally follow. A strong spirit is what carries you through times of suffering, confusion and chaos. Just as a master is like the mountain that holds steady amidst a chaotic and changing world, a strong spirit is the grounding force in your personal character.

Our spirit is the part of us that never dies. Our spirit is the part of us that remains connected to the Universe always, like a winding river that eventually spills into the ocean.

Meditation will show you your spirit. Meditation can be formal or informal. You can learn techniques to practice a particular discipline, or you can just be still and listen to your breath. You can meditate as part of a specific spiritual pathway, or you can do it as part of your complete experience of life apart from any special practice. If you want to have a small glimpse of the peace and the beauty meditation can open you up to, try this:

Quiet your thoughts, if you can. Listen inside your head for a deep silence, beneath the chatter of your mind and the sounds of the ordinary world. Hear that quiet as you would listen to the sound of the ocean inside the shell of a conch. That is the sound of the Universe. Listen carefully enough, silently enough, patiently enough, and you will begin to feel a penetrating and awesome sense of well-being, and eventually, joy.

This expansive silence never leaves us. We have just learned to tune it out. We concentrate on the industrial wheels grinding along, the humming and honking of cars, people shouting, our thoughts banging around in our heads like pots and lids crashing – and in all the clamor, we miss the most exquisite music. In the most unbearable of all moments, all we need to do is shut off the noise and we will hear this music, feel this peace.

In the midst of this peace, this ocean of quietude, we can feel that nothing really matters. We are not really so important. The vastness of the Universe, the perfection of nature and Her continuous cycles dwarfs all of our little sufferings and dealings with their foreverness. Older people know: nothing lasts. No happiness lasts forever, no pain lasts forever. All things, all events, all feelings from this world, are transient. The quiet inside our minds – that is the only thing that is forever, changeless, eternal. The closer we can get to experiencing that eternal part of us, the more we will remain unmoved by the daily highs and lows of our existence.

One day something great happens – we're happy. The next day something unpleasant happens – we're sad. Happy, sad, frustrated, satiated, excited, bored. It never ends. Our changing circumstances will never change.

But *we* can. The key is having a strong spirit. The key is connecting to that inner quiet, that deep awareness that there is a part of each of us that is eternal. We do this through meditation. Meditation is the quieting of the mind, the exploration of the silence behind and beyond our thoughts.

There are many different techniques you can learn, but all of the techniques have as a foundation the stopping of one's thoughts.

When we think of meditation, sometimes we think of Asian monks in ochre colored robes, or statues of the Buddha. In fact, nearly every culture has some tradition of meditation and the practice is not as obscure as one might think. In the West, popular American philosophers like Henry David Thoreau and Ralph Waldo Emerson have written about the importance of self-reflection since the turn of the last century. Meditation is not just for monks. It is not limited to any particular religion or spiritual path. Meditation is for every person who is interested in living a happier life. Meditation is particularly helpful for practitioners of The Three-Fold Path to Mastery, who seek superior levels of self-control in order to provide the best possible service to others.

We have discussed the importance of seeming unmoved by change – how it helps others to trust you and to be able to depend on you. Why not *actually be* unmoved by change?

Meditation will give you a strong spirit. A strong spirit will ground you in the exquisite and eternal force of the Universe. Experiencing firsthand the force of the Universe will give you a deep sense of contentment and overriding joy. This deep sense of joy will be accessible always, giving you a unique perspective on your shifting moods and experiences, rendering all phenomena of the world trivial in comparison to your ecstasy.

No matter what the circumstances in your life, no matter how joyous or how tragic, if you draw your happiness and peace from within your mind, you will always feel happy and at peace.

There is no greater way to increase your store of energy, or raise your personal power, than to find an endless source of power inside yourself.

Every moment of your life is another opportunity to engage your spirit in the thrill of existence. You have the choice, at any moment, whether to gain energy or lose it. You have control over whether you will have personal power or not. As a Warrior, you decide in each and every moment of your life, whether you will be ordinary or extraordinary, average or a master.

CHAPTER SUMMARY

WARRIOR TRAINING

- Warrior Training involves the non-violent methods for reaching extraordinary heights of achievement and happiness, based on different ways to modify and monitor mental and physical activity throughout each day.
- Being a Warrior means accepting responsibility for your life.
- To be a warrior, you must cultivate a strong body, a strong mind, and a strong spirit:
    - Develop a strong body through exercise. Martial arts, yoga, and running/hiking/walking are particularly good forms of exercise for increasing your personal power as well as your stamina.
    - Develop a strong mind by stimulating it with new information, and by forcing it to learn, expand, and change.
    - Develop a strong spirit through the practice of meditation.

CHAPTER EXERCISES

WARRIOR TRAINING

1. Strong Body

a) Set a new goal: Overcoming physical limitations can be a powerful metaphor for overcoming even more profound challenges. To feel this for yourself, set an exercise goal to achieve at the end of one week. Make the goal just beyond what you think you can do. For example, if you normally jog two miles a day, work up to jogging three and a half miles one day before the end of the next week. Even a small achievement like this can significantly alter your view of yourself and your abilities.

b) Stand with power: The basic stance for beginning training in Japanese karate is called "Fudo Dachi" or "ready stance." This is a strong standing pose that prepares the body and mind for the discipline of practice.

   i) Stand with your feet shoulder width apart, toes pointing 45 degrees outward.

   ii) Bend your knees slightly, tuck your rear end in, lift your ribs up and out and push your shoulders back.

   iii) Form your hands into fists by curling your pinky finger under, then the rest of your fingers, wrapping your thumb around the outside of your first. Hold your arms at your sides, angled slightly away from your body.

   iv) Tuck your chin in gently and look straight ahead.

   v) Breathe in deeply through your nose. Despite the strength you are bringing to standing this way, try not to clench anything tightly. You must be relaxed in order to jump into action quickly and precisely.

vi) Take a few slow, deep breaths and remind yourself that power is not conferred by anyone outside of you. You bring power up from the depths of your being.

vii) Practice this stance in the morning to get yourself charged up for a day of inner combat against the forces of laziness and dishonesty.

2. *Strong Mind*

a) This week, determine to learn something new. Buy a book about ikebana or Chaos Theory or beginning French.

b) Read a few pages every day. Even this minor investment of time spent absorbing significantly new information than what you are normally exposed to will stimulate your brain and help you to think about problems and solutions in innovative ways.

3. *Strong Spirit*

In this Key, as well as in Key #10, *Focus,* we explored some simple meditation techniques. Here is another non-denominational technique for quieting the mind and entering a state of peace and effortless joy.

a) Purchase the most exquisite flower you can find and place it in a vase, or locate a photograph of a flower that is equally appealing to you.

b) Sit down in a quiet place away from activity or noise. Ideally, you should find a clean room at home where you can close the door and feel safe and undisturbed.

c) You can sit any way you feel comfortable, either cross-legged on a pillow on the floor, on a chair, or on a velvet throne...whatever works for you. Just make sure your back is completely straight.

d) Gaze at the flower or the photograph of a flower in front of you. Slow your breathing. Notice the shape and distinct coloring of every petal. See how the leaves lean from the stem.

e) After a minute or two, close your eyes. Try to see the flower inside your mind. Hold the image as long as you can, keeping your breath slow and even. Strive not to form thoughts or descriptive words about the flower. Just see it, witness it innocently, without judgment, without adjectives.

f) Rest like this as long as you can. If the mental picture of the flower fades, reconstruct it with your imagination, without opening your eyes. The details may fade, but a sense of the flower's shape and color can still remain as a feeling, apart from any picture.

g) As mentioned in Key #10, it is always nice to have a moment of gratitude following a period of meditation, no matter how brief. Just close your eyes and think, "Thank you." Bow if that feels comfortable to you. Meditation and the gift of even a single moment of peace is a privilege that merits being acknowledged by these simple gestures.

KEY #16: CONCLUDING AN ASSIGNMENT

"And shall it be said that my eve was in truth my dawn?"
– Kahlil Gibran

A flute plays a quiet tune. The hero of a Hollywood Western has just put down the last of the bad guys. Townspeople are gathered around, shaken, grateful. Dust swirls in the air. Spurs jangling, the hero mounts his horse and rides off, not looking back. The setting sun, massive on the horizon, frames the silhouette of the hero as he disappears in the gold light. Back in town people return to business as usual, bodies cleared from the square, the immediate threat gone.

Everyone loves a hero. We all wish we could be the best at something, whether that is giving a funny and rousing speech, writing precise computer code, playing a musical instrument, analyzing stock performance, helping a failing business become profitable, or knocking off the bad guys. Heroes do their job, then inevitably, they ride off leaving no trace. We all have the potential to be heroes. Most of us never realize that potential. A master rides off into the sunset, as grateful colleagues go on with their business, the immediate problem solved.

In this Key, I will share with you surprisingly unknown and underused methods for building an extremely favorable reputation, getting colleagues and managers to provide you with impressive references, and for ensuring unlimited future work opportunities.

Concluding an assignment is one of the areas where even otherwise conscientious people show a surprising lack of etiquette and prevent a perfectly good work experience from leading to future ones. In fact, one of the biggest gripes in the business world is that people do such an incredibly poor job of closing down their projects, assignments and work.

Full-time jobs, consulting assignments or projects can end for many reasons, including:

- A company initiative is cancelled, postponed, or completed
- The agreed goal, deliverable or contract duration is reached
- You choose to resign
- Funding runs out
- Your performance is unsatisfactory

Regardless of how your work experience terminates, you should always handle the last few weeks, days or hours with great care. While first impressions are important for setting the tone of your future relationships, last impressions can be extremely influential in people's memories once you have ended your work with them.

How To Properly Conclude Your Assignment

The conclusion of a job, project or assignment is where you have one of the best opportunities to demonstrate a commitment to service. Here is how a typical person will end his assignments:

- Files are left as is – with papers and old file folders forgotten.
- Voice mail is left untouched. The red light signaling messages can remain on a telephone for weeks until the telecommunications department is able to reassign the number. In the meantime, associates who don't know that the person has left wonder why no one has returned their calls.
- Proprietary knowledge the person gained while working for his company, or on his projects or assignments, is not discussed or shared with anyone else, leaving a gap in understanding for others to figure out once he has gone. He probably didn't leave forwarding information, so his former employer has no simple way of getting hold of the information he may desperately need.

- Virtually no one is aware that he has left his job or assignment until weeks later.
- Months after his departure, he calls one of his former managers or colleagues asking for a reference, though he never even said goodbye to them when he was leaving the company.

Some of these problems are not entirely the fault of the individual. A good manager or employer will alert others that one of his staff is leaving and will take steps to ensure that no knowledge is lost once that person has departed. Nevertheless, it is always wise to assume responsibility and cover all the bases ourselves.

Here is a checklist of the activities you should always perform prior to leaving any job, project or assignment, regardless of the circumstances:

- *Thank people.* Make a list, if necessary, of all the people who were helpful to you during your work at the company or on the project. Visit colleagues with whom you worked closely and thank each of them in person. Also send each additional person on your list, individually, a message or note, thanking him for his help. If the person is senior, you may want to ask him to be a reference for you (see *Get References* below). If the person is junior, copy the message to the person's direct manager. You'll be doing him a favor and he will appreciate the kind gesture.
- *Clean up.* Clean up your work area. Throw out old papers and align the phone, computer, mouse and other items on the desk. Throw out the cartoons you pinned to the cubicle wall and remove any speed dial labels you taped on the phone.
- *Organize paper files.* Throw out papers, documents and files that are duplicated elsewhere or are insignificant. Identify the documents and files which may be important or which may be needed in the future. Ask for guidelines on what documents need to be saved. Never discard original or unique documents unless directed to do so.
- *Organize electronic files.* Go through your personal and network directories and identify files that need to be stored for future reference or audit purposes. Store important files in

logically named folders (use real, meaningful, English words –
not cryptic abbreviations that no one will be able to decipher)
on a network directory that your colleagues have access to.
Again, ask for some guidance on what files need to be saved.

- *Delete personal files.* Once you have saved the files you needed to, or were required to, delete *every single* file or program
that you created personally, and that you saved or installed on
the computer's hard drive and on your personal network drive,
without the approval or knowledge of the IT department. Yes,
most companies' computer departments will normally clean
out a computer after you leave and before a new person is
assigned to use it. Clean it out anyway.

If you've been diligent in maintaining your computer, it
won't be that big a job for you. If not, it's worth the effort. You
don't want to leave open the possibility of any document you
created being left on the computer for someone else to find.
The files that are inadvertently left on a hard drive are usually
personal. You probably don't want anyone to find these.
(Though after reading Key #12, *Work Etiquette,* you may have
stopped saving personal files on your office PC.) Sometimes
computers get moved around within a company; even if the
document is not personal, it might be proprietary to your manager, project or department.

Leaving electronic files around after ending an assignment
is like leaving a messy desk. It's not polite. It's sloppy. Real professionals clean up messes, they don't create them.

- *Prune e-mail.* Most of your messages should be deleted before
you leave. However, you may need to archive some messages
identified as potentially relevant for a future audit.

- *Transfer knowledge.* Identify any knowledge you may have gained
while you were working at the company, or on the project or
assignment, which may not be known to others. Explain to a manager your interest in ensuring that this information be transferred
to someone who will be remaining on the job. This gesture will be
greatly appreciated. Offer to write a document containing the
information, or to train selected staff over a short period of time.

- *Get references.* Identify colleagues whom you would feel comfortable providing you with a professional reference. Meet with each person if possible, rather than just sending notes or e-mail. Bring a letter to the meeting typed on good-quality paper requesting a reference. Mention how much you would value his support and how much you enjoyed working with him during this past assignment. If handled correctly, people you have asked to provide references often become people who sing your praises after you are gone or who contact you about future opportunities. Be extremely polite and don't react badly if the person for some reason declines to provide you with a reference. Accept any response with a smile and your sincere good wishes for the future.

  Some companies don't allow staff to provide endorsements of anyone by writing reference letters. This is a shame, but can sometimes be circumvented by using e-mail instead. With a manager's approval, ask people to send you a message thanking you for your efforts, being as specific as possible. You can then print out the e-mail and hold onto it for your records.

- *Bring your work home.* Identify any documents or presentations you created while you were working of which you are particularly proud. Ask permission to retain a copy for your personal records. If acceptable, bring the files home and place them in a folder or binder, which will in time become a personal portfolio of your best work. You can use this portfolio during interviews as evidence of the breadth of your abilities.

Personal Assessment

Once you have completed an assignment, set aside time to reflect by yourself. Consider ways you could improve your work, and your actions. Make a chart with the headings: *Done Well* and *Could Be Improved*. Don't just beat yourself up with all the mistakes you think you made. You should also remind yourself of all the good things you did and all the reasons why you are on your way to becoming an even greater success on your next project. You will need to be objective, optimistic and confident of your abilities in order to triumph. Humility, if you recall, is seeing things exactly as they are: no better and no worse. Humbly recognize all your wins, as well as your more modest achievements and your defeats.

For items you've noted in the *Could Be Improved* column, actively seek out ways to have these items listed in the *Done Well* column following your next job or project. Perhaps you need to take a class in public speaking to better prepare yourself for presentations. Perhaps you need to work on your people skills, or typing. Perhaps you simply need to gain more experience in your field. Follow up. So few people do!

Professional Assessment

If you are really brave, schedule a closing meeting with your manager and ask him to provide you with an objective assessment of your work. Explain that you are always seeking to improve your skills in all areas, and that you would be grateful for his feedback. Assure him that you are equally interested in negative feedback and that he should be honest with you in order to really help you out.

Ask him: "Are you happy with the work I've done for you?" "Why?" or "Why not?" And, "Can you help me identify areas where I need to improve?"

Most people will be very surprised, and impressed, at your request for feedback. They will be even more surprised and impressed when you handle any negative comments with humility and grace.

The senior program manager for a contract I worked on asked me for a professional assessment of his performance towards the conclusion of an intensive organizational change project. He had been my senior on the contract and I was stunned that he was allowing me this opportunity to provide him with the feedback I had been, frankly, too shy to share with him during our work together. He was an exceptionally talented consultant, but his military training (we all assumed) had left him reserved and perfunctory. We never knew where we stood with him and he would often work in near-total isolation. I felt these were areas for improvement, but nevertheless I had a great amount of respect for his abilities and his obviously high intelligence. We met in his office and I shared my thoughts. He looked me in the eye while I was speaking. He took notes! I could see that even though I had been trying to say everything with kindness, some of my points struck a nerve. Nevertheless, he thanked me sincerely following our meeting.

At the time I could only imagine how impressed the client we were consulting to must have been when he approached them with the same request. Since I started asking for assessments from my colleagues and employers, I have been amazed by the power of this act of service (and bravery). It is always a bit unnerving when you walk into an assessment meeting, but the rewards are significant. Mainly, you are given the information you need to avoid making the same mistakes twice, and to ensure you improve with each new assignment.

At the end of an assessment meeting, always conclude the conversation on a positive note. Tell your manager or colleague something like, "Thank you so much for your time and for your honesty. I feel very positive about this experience and I am grateful that I was able to help you achieve your goals." Let your last statement be a reminder of the most positive aspect of your work on the project. Imagine good feelings, and both of your smiles, lingering in the air after you've left the meeting room.

If you embrace the philosophy of The Three-Fold Path to Mastery, you will not only be doing good work for people. You will probably be an agent of change: improving businesses as well as peoples' lives. During your employment or throughout a project you always treat others with respect, you work with focus and discipline and you adhere to the highest ethical principles. Inevitably you will leave a business better off, in one way or another, than when you started. Gratitude and applause are not necessary. You'll know in your heart, each day you leave the office, that you offered the best of yourself to your work. Regardless of any specific outcome of your efforts, your service was complete. It is each day that matters, not the grand finale.

Nevertheless, prepare each day for your Hollywood exit. Then you can ride off into the sunset at a moment's notice, a hero for the hour, without the laborious burden of regret.

CHAPTER SUMMARY

CONCLUDING AN ASSIGNMENT

- Prepare for the conclusion of your work the day you start. If you maintain order in your files and personal effects, you will not have to expend a lot of effort to close them down.
- Be respectful of the people you may be leaving behind: tend to your voice mail, paper and electronic files, and arrange to transfer knowledge to others.
- Do a personal assessment of your efforts:
  - Create a chart with columns for *Done Well* and *Could Be Improved*
  - Follow up on weak areas, don't just ignore them
- Schedule a meeting with your manager for a professional assessment of your efforts:
  - Explain how valuable feedback is to you
  - Assure the manager that you are equally as interested in negative feedback as in positive comments
  - Thank the person and always end the meeting on a positive note

CHAPTER EXERCISES

CONCLUDING AN ASSIGNMENT

1. Personal Assessment

Without the immediate threat of being scrutinized, you are going to prepare a personal assessment chart for practice, to help you gain perspective on the quality of your current efforts.

a) Get a legal pad or other piece of paper and make a line down the center. Create a heading on the left side of the line called "Done Well." On the right side of the line create a header called "Could Be Improved."

b) Imagine that you are leaving your current employment today. With the clarity of hindsight start filling in the columns on your sheet. From the first day of your job to the present, what are the things that you did particularly well? List these things in the left side column. What are your areas for improvement? List these in the right side column. Don't make your answers too general – list specific examples of things you could have done better.

c) Read through your "Done Well" column. Is there a pattern? Are you good at organization, for example, but less talented at running meetings? Are you good at expressing yourself over the phone, but find it impossible to write coherently?

d) Read through your "Could Be Improved" column. Are there any patterns you notice from your entries on this side of the page?

e) Try to group your answers into categories (which may have been revealed through your look at patterns), for example: Interpersonal skills, Conflict resolution, Organization, Strategy, etc.

Hopefully this exercise revealed your major problem areas, as well as your skills. Now consider what changes you can make as a result of what was revealed from the items listed in your "Could Be Improved" column. Don't just compile this list and put it away. Take action. Before you end the exercise, brainstorm a few ideas for how to eliminate one of these areas from your right-side list. Then, take one small action towards improving yourself in one category. Taking one small action after another will result in significant transformation over time. Start now. Positive change will happen, sooner than you think.

KEY #17: INTERVIEWING

"Service to others is the rent you pay for your room here on Earth."

— *Muhammad Ali*

The prospect of an interview can be exciting, but it is also usually fraught with anxiety. If you are like most people, you probably approach interviews with such powerlessness you might actually be better off allowing an employer to evaluate you on paper alone. Sound shocking?

In this Key, you will be introduced to specific and extremely effective techniques for shifting the power dynamic of an interview in your favor, and for making a convincing and dazzling impression that will outshine other candidates who take an ordinary approach to the job selection process.

There are two major differences between the *art* of interviewing on The Three-Fold Path to Mastery, and the *act* of interviewing for the average person. One difference is in your overall approach, and the other difference is in the details of your preparation and presentation.

Let's start with the approach. You are probably under the assumption that the interviewer holds your fate in his hands. If this is true, then on your big day you will dress your best, shake his hand with your slightly clammy palm, try to smile a bit, answer his questions and then leave with your heart in your throat wondering how you did. Perhaps you may even glance nervously around the elevators as you leave, exploring the office for other candidates waiting for their turn in the fire.

This type of feeble interview experience is extremely common, and completely unnecessary. There is absolutely no need to turn a potentially powerful situation into a mewing, obsequious popularity contest.

Consider the reason you have been asked to interview for a particular job: the company has a need for someone with a specific set of skills, and you possess these skills to a reasonable degree. They have a need, and you have the solution. Whether you are an expert in your field or not, you are clearly more of an expert than anyone the company has available, or they wouldn't need to hire you. This is the key. *They* need *you*. It is so simple and yet most people overlook this fact when preparing for an interview. Thus, the right way to approach the experience is from a position of power: to look at it as a *meeting* rather than as an *interview*.

Try to stop looking at the process as a tool for your potential employer's benefit alone, and recognize that it is equally a chance for you to decide whether you are interested in working for the company.

If you are endeavoring to put into practice all the techniques of The Three-Fold Path to Mastery – constantly learning new skills, continuing your education, gaining experience in your field in novel ways and bringing the best of yourself to each moment – then the employer should consider hiring you a great opportunity. You are going to bring an attitude of selflessness to your activities for the company, when a large percentage of everyone else working for them probably maintains an attitude of selfishness. Your ability and willingness to remain focused on your work throughout the day makes you significantly more productive and less likely to make mistakes than most others. Bring this recognition of your value with you when you interact with a prospective company. Hold it in your mind, as if you were browsing in a jewelry store and you knew you had $30,000 in cash in your pocket.

A meeting is a coming together of equals to discuss solutions and goals. You will know you have succeeded in cultivating the correct attitude when you notice the employer trying to *sell you* on working for *them*.

In addition to having the right approach, there are a few precise and powerful techniques you can use to significantly improve your chances of making an unforgettable impression on your employer. Basic and obvious interviewing techniques that have already been presented in numerous other books will not be repeated here. Rather, we are going to cover some distinctly non-ordinary methods that you may never have read about before, concerning your presentation and preparation for the big meeting.

Dress Flawlessly

We considered the art of appearance in the beginning of this book. When preparing for your preliminary meeting, you must ensure that your appearance is flawless, whether it is appropriate for you to be wearing casual clothes or an Armani suit. This does not just mean wearing a clean outfit, but taking your appearance to military boot camp levels of perfection. Chase every detail. For example, check for loose threads hanging off a button or lapel; iron out every last wrinkle from the fabric; choose clean, unscuffed shoes that don't have extreme signs of wear around the heel and make sure they are polished to a sheen if they are made of smooth leather; women and men should have tidy, clean nails. As we covered in Key #2, *Acting As If,* you will be wearing the most expensive business clothes you were able to afford.

Your appearance will soundlessly communicate a message to those you encounter. In an interview you will be scrutinized head to toe. This is an opportunity to take back the power of yet another aspect of the experience. You will strategically use your appearance to convey two very important qualities to the interviewer:

- You are precise, meticulous, detail-oriented
- You are highly successful

The first quality shows the interviewer that you can do a job thoroughly and that you can be trusted to be left alone while you work. Executives and managers love this! The last thing the person hiring you wants is to have to supervise your work when he is probably already too busy to get his own work done. The second quality demonstrates that you are so good at what you do that you are compensated on the higher end of your position's typical salary range. This allows you to convincingly ask for the highest salary or rate you deserve and get it. The employer won't want to lose you to another company!

Stalk the Company

One way to improve your chance of getting hired immediately is to "stalk" the company, the day or the week before your interview. "Stalking" means exactly what it sounds like – stalk the company like a wild animal hunting prey.[xxxviii]

First, as suggested in Key #11, *Politics & Strategy*, learn basic information about the company. You can probably find what you need on the internet. If not, try to obtain a recent annual report. How is the company doing financially? Has it recently been acquired or has it recently merged with or acquired another company? What is its bond rating? Learn where the company fits in the larger business picture. Is it a manufacturer, a retailer, a professional services firm, etc.? Locate the company's mission statement if you can. If the person you will be meeting with is a company officer or executive, see if any biographies of this person are available on the company's website.

Once you are armed with this data, you are ready to begin stalking. At least one day prior to your interview, go to the office building where the company is located and stand outside at lunch hour. Watch the people go in and out of the building. (If the office building is home to more than one company, try to get yourself up to the right floor, or in some way identify just the people who work for the company you are stalking.)

Notice what the people are wearing. Try to sense what it is like to work for this company by the way its employees walk, by the expressions on their faces as they leave for lunch, by their overall appearance. Are they in khakis or suits? Do they seem quiet or gregarious? Do they look miserable or focused?

This is not an exercise for your logical mind. This is an exercise in being able to intuit something non-obvious about your next potential employer. Like the hunter who has stalked his prey so closely he can predict the animal's every move, sense where it will hunt and sleep and nest, try to *sense* what it means to be an employee of this company. A hunter who has carefully stalked his prey can actually move as if he were the prey. He can act so much like the prey itself, he becomes indistinguishable from it. As such, he becomes non-threatening and can even approach the prey up close without scaring it away.

You must stalk the company and its staff so well, that you can easily pass as one of them. When you arrive for your interview, you must *Act As If* you were already working for this company. Project an impression that you *belong* there. Your behavior must be subtle. Don't try to pull this off superficially or you will appear silly and manipulative. If you want to work for this company badly enough, and if you have done your research, then your behavior will naturally take on the characteristics of this company's current employees.

This exercise isn't as simple as it might seem, but with practice it will become much easier and more fluid. One of the qualities employers look for first is whether you will fit in with the other staff members or with the team. However, on a deeper level, what you are doing by stalking the company is presenting the employer with the "after" picture, even though you are still technically a "before." You are communicating subtly that you are a natural fit with the environment, assisting the interviewer in coming to that conclusion himself.

Monitor Body Language

Plenty has already been written about body language, and the interview technique of "mirroring," so we will just touch upon this briefly. Mirroring means that if your interviewer leans forward as he is speaking, you do the same. If he sits back in his chair and crosses his legs, you follow. The idea is that, if done with some subtlety, by mirroring your interviewer's body language, you give the impression of being like-minded. He will pick up on some level that you understand each other. He will then feel warmly towards you because you are like him.

Mirroring someone's body language just for the sake of it, simply because you read somewhere it was a good idea, is a bad idea. You will probably be found out and will look manipulative. Mirroring works when you aren't trying to do it. When you are listening to your interviewer carefully and truly attempting to understand this person's needs, so that you can be of service to him and to his company, your body language will naturally have some symmetry. It is a very good sign when you notice that mirroring is occurring without artificial maneuvering.

Nevertheless, you should always be aware of hidden messages your own body language may be sending. We all have a natural tendency to cross our arms over our chest when we are upset, angry or when we disagree with a point being made. It's a protective reflex. It has no place in an interview. Here, you want to convey a sense of open-mindedness, of comfortable confidence. Keep your arms resting on the arms of your chair, folded or clasped in your lap. The key is to keep them open and not crossed.

Notice if your interviewer suddenly crosses his arms over his chest, and/or crosses his legs. You must be saying something that he doesn't like, finds threatening, or disagrees with. Find some way to renegotiate the point. Change your tone of voice. Use his body language as a gauge of how well your interview is going and as an immediate warning sign of when you need to turn it around.

Present a Portfolio of Work

The *pièce de résistance* of your interview, other than your own fabulous appearance, wise commentary and quiet charm, is your portfolio. For this, you will need a black three-ring binder with a clear cover and heavyweight sheet protectors. Print your name in 16-point bold font in the center of a page and then put the page into a clear sleeve in the front of the binder, so your name shows through the cover.

Insert your resume into sheet protectors and insert these pages into the binder following your cover page. (Note that you should bring a fresh copy of your resume to every interview, in addition to the copy that will remain in your portfolio, even if you know the person you're meeting with already has a copy. Your resume should be printed on the highest quality paper – the kind that practically stands up by itself. Use a laser printer to avoid the cheaper look you can get from ink jet printers.)

Now you can get creative. Include anything in your portfolio that establishes you as an expert in your field:

- Have you won awards or certificates?
- Have you published articles?
- Have articles been written about you?
- Do you have reference letters on particularly impressive letter-

head (i.e., from Fortune 500 corporations or written by a company CEO)?

- Do you have any other letters of commendation, on letterhead or in e-mail form?

If you are not yet an expert, try to find information to insert into your portfolio that distinguishes you:

- Have you received a compliment from a previous employer in an e-mail?
- Have you done volunteer work? Do you have photos of your experiences?

If you do not have anything that would go in your binder yet, consider your portfolio incentive to start accumulating material that establishes you as an expert in your field and/or that distinguishes you as a unique achiever in other areas.

Once your portfolio has a few pages other than your resume, you are ready to bring it with you to an interview. Place it on the desk along with your business card, if you have one, once you've been introduced to your interviewer. Suggest that if he has time, you would love to walk him through parts of your resume and background that are applicable to the position you will be discussing.

A portfolio is just as impressive for the fact that you've put in the effort to create one, as it is for its contents. The night before an interview, or a few minutes before as you wait for your meeting to start, review your own binder. Read through your resume and flip through the plastic sleeves displaying your accomplishments and honors.

If you ever have moments of doubt in your abilities, moments where your confidence wavers, where you question whether you really are worth the salary or position you are asking for, allow yourself to indulge momentarily in this career review. Let it remind you that you *are* worth higher compensation than most other people in your field. Let it remind you of all the work you do to ensure that most of your actions during your assignments end up in the *Done Well* column of your personal assessment. (Reread Key #16, *Concluding an Assignment,* to refresh your memory about the personal assessment exercise.)

Your portfolio is a manifestation of your personal power. Carry this binder around as an expression of the exceptional way you live your life and direct your career.

Approach your *meeting* with your prospective employer with the intention of helping this person solve a particular problem. You are in the business of providing service. Listen intently as the interviewer describes the position, the problem the position was created to address and his role in finding the solution. Is there a problem underlying the obvious one being discussed? If you listen carefully enough, sometimes you can hear things that help you understand your interviewer more deeply. This is a human being who needs help. Are you the one who can take away some of his pain?

We are fortunate to be in the position to help others. Be compassionate. Use all the skills you've developed for putting your own issues aside in order to better focus on your interviewer's needs.

What you will invariably find is that when you put aside your problems to help others with theirs, your concerns fade into insignificance. By helping others, you end up feeling better.

A first meeting or interview is no more than a consultation, during which someone shares a problem with you in the hope that you can help him solve it. This is a moment of pure service. Don't let your anxiety about the meeting, your insecurity about your abilities, or other emotions, detract from the perfection of this brief time when you can demonstrate what service really means.

Enjoy this opportunity to exchange information and practice your people skills. Then, even if you don't get the job, the time you spent preparing for the interview is never wasted. Don't be so focused on the end result – getting the job – that you miss the fun of the chase or the chance to practice your pathway to mastery.

APPENDIX TO KEY #17

It's always helpful not to take ourselves too seriously. Now that we have considered the right way to approach interviews, let's have some fun and look at some, shall we say, less conventional methods...

Vice Presidents and personnel directors of the one hundred largest corporations in the U.S. were asked to describe their most unusual experience interviewing prospective employees. Here are some of their incredible replies:[xxxix]

- Job applicant challenged the interviewer to an arm wrestle.
- Applicant wore a Walkman, explaining that she could listen to the interviewer and the music at the same time.
- Candidate fell and broke arm during interview.
- Candidate announced she hadn't had lunch and proceeded to eat a hamburger and french fries in the interviewer's office.
- Candidate explained that her long-term goal was to replace the interviewer.
- Candidate said he never finished high school because he was kidnapped and kept in a closet in Mexico.
- Balding candidate excused himself and returned to the office a few minutes later wearing a hairpiece.
- Applicant said if he were hired he would demonstrate his loyalty by having the corporate logo tattooed on his forearm.
- Applicant interrupted interview to phone her therapist for advice on how to answer specific interview questions.
- Candidate brought large dog to interview.

The employers were also asked to list the most unusual questions that job candidates had posed. Here are some of their entries:

- "What is it that you people do at this company?"
- "Why aren't you in a more interesting business?"
- "What are the zodiac signs of all the board members?"
- "Why do you want references?"
- "I know this is off the subject, but will you marry me?"
- "Will the company move my rock collection from California to Maryland?"

- "Will the company pay to relocate my horse?"
- "Does your health insurance cover pets?"
- "Would it be a problem if I'm angry most of the time?"
- "Does your company have a policy regarding concealed weapons?"
- "Do you think the company would be willing to lower my pay?"
- "Why am I here?"

Finally, the employers were asked to share unusual statements made by candidates during the interview process:

- "I have no difficulty in starting or holding my bowel movement."
- "At times I have the strong urge to do something harmful or shocking."
- "I feel uneasy indoors."
- "Sometimes I feel like smashing things."
- "Once a week, I usually feel hot all over."
- "I am fascinated by fire."
- "Whenever a man is with a woman he is usually thinking about sex."
- "People are always watching me."
- "Almost everyone is guilty of bad sexual conduct."
- "I never get hungry."
- "I know who is responsible for most of my troubles."
- "If the pay was right, I'd travel with the carnival."
- "I would have been more successful if nobody would have snitched on me."
- "My legs are really hairy."
- "I think I'm going to throw-up."

Chapter Summary

Interviewing

- Approach your interview from a position of power, not weakness:
  - Recognize your value to the company
  - Remember that meetings with employers are as much for your benefit, as for theirs
- Dress flawlessly to convey two important qualities:
  - You are precise, meticulous, detail-oriented
  - You are extremely successful
- Stalk the company:
  - Find out informative details, such as specifics about the industry as well as the company's financial status
  - Stalk the employees to understand what it is like to work there
  - Make the interviewer feel as though you already work for the company
- Monitor body language
- Prepare and present a portfolio of your accomplishments
- Don't forget to enjoy the interview process, and learn from the experience, regardless of the outcome

CHAPTER EXERCISES

INTERVIEWING

1. Embrace Your Power: Creating Your Personal Power Document

This exercise may assist you in improving your resume; however, it is also intended to help you understand clearly what distinguishes you as a job candidate and as an individual. Believing in your power is vital when you arrive at your meeting with an interviewer. It is also a great leap forward in feeling content with your choices and your life.

a) On a blank piece of paper make a list of your last three job titles, or your three most significant assignments if you have been working in the same position for more than five years. Allow each of the sections to take up a third of the page.

   i) Under each section, list all the accomplishments you are proud of that you achieved during each job or assignment. List successful projects you were involved with, compliments you received from superiors or colleagues, and/or moments when you felt you made a difference.

   ii) Are there any items from this list that you can add to your resume?

b) On another blank piece of paper make a list of the following:

   i) Other languages you speak, or that you studied in school

   ii) Any hobbies you have, or had, in which you have invested significant time

   iii) Sports in which you have won awards or otherwise distinguished yourself

iv) Musical instruments you play, or used to play. Singing also counts, though not if it was confined to the shower or the car...

v) Any instance when you appeared or when you were interviewed on radio, TV or in print, apart from school newspapers

vi) Any presentations you have given, to more than three people, for any reason

vii) Volunteer or charity work you have performed, or supported

vii) Teaching or tutoring you have done "on the side"

Are there any items from these lists that you could add to your resume?

c) Think carefully: have you had any experiences that are not ordinary and that you handled in an interesting way?

i) Did you ever save somebody's life?

ii) Did you have a devastating experience and survive?

iii) Did you ever meet a particularly fascinating celebrity? A world leader, for example, or a brilliant mathematician like Dr. John Nash?

iv) Were you born in a foreign country? Did you grow up in Alaska, or on a farm, or in a penthouse, or in a commune?

d) Now, type up your answers from sections "a" through "c" and read them over. Consider all the interesting and unique experiences you have had. If you can see a way to add some of your distinguishing experiences and talents to your resume, do this now. Even if you don't add anything to your resume, you can still make great use out of your Personal Power Document. Chances are that other candidates for your position have very different backgrounds than you. Whether your skills are better or not doesn't matter. What is important is that you recognize the areas where you stand out.

e) Reflect on how items from your lists add to your qualifications to do your job well. For example, if you once volunteered in a home for senior citizens and listened to their stories, perhaps this makes you a better manager, since the experience taught you patience, caring and listening to others' needs. On a new piece of paper, make a list of three to five items from any of your previous lists, and describe how each one has broadened your horizons or how it gives you unusual depth or ability in your chosen profession.

f) If you found that any of your lists for sections "a", "b" and "c" had fewer than two entries, don't feel discouraged! Now you have a checklist for the types of activities you can get involved with that will enhance your professional profile, add to your confidence and deepen your character.

The next time you schedule a meeting with a prospective employer, make sure to read through your Personal Power Document, and remember how much value you can share with this company. Keep adding to your document when you have new "wins." During times of challenge or low self esteem, print out a copy and post it on your bathroom mirror as a reminder of how special you are and how much progress you continue to make on The Three-Fold Path to Mastery.

2. *Getting the Look*

Before you can put together the perfect interview outfit, you need to know very specifically what image you are trying to project. Remember the axiom - you don't want to dress for the job you have, but for the job you are trying to get. This may involve shopping. It definitely will involve stalking. Here's the exercise:

a) Depending upon your industry, buy a trade magazine that publishes articles and photographs of people that excel in your field. Flip through the pictures until you get an idea of the average style of your profession's superstars. Now, extrapolate for your job level. The head of your department might come to work wearing Versace, but you can find comparable styles in less expensive labels. Ultimately, you will want to save up and buy an expensive suit like the head of a department wears. One day, that job could be yours!

b) Go to lunch in an area of town where people from your industry often meet. In New York, for example, certain neighborhoods and restaurants are well-known "hangouts" for publishing, advertising, fashion, politics, and so on. Find out where to go, bring a notepad, and take notes: What are your colleagues wearing? How do they carry themselves? What kind of briefcase are they carrying?

c) At home, review your closet. Can you put together a suitable interview outfit from what you already own? It's always good to wear something new to an interview, because it gives you a feeling of being different than the person who had your previous job. If you cannot purchase an entirely new outfit for your meeting, still try to purchase one new thing to wear: a scarf, a tie, even a new pair of socks. In new clothes there are no memories of what you did when you wore them before. You are a new person getting a new start!

3. *Practicing the Walk and the Talk*

Invite a friend out to dinner and ask him to "play" interviewer for you. Dress the part and be willing to hear constructive criticism politely. Explain the general requirements of the position you are seeking and ask your friend to honestly evaluate your responses, your body language, your mannerisms and even your outfit. You may be surprised what signals you are giving out without realizing it!

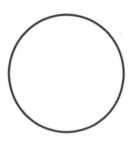

THE THIRD PATHWAY

THE CIRCLE

*"One can have no smaller or greater mastery
than mastery of oneself."*
– Leonardo da Vinci

KEY #18: MASTERY

"Without fear, go.
Meditate. Live purely. Be quiet.
Do your work with mastery.
Never offend, by what you say or think or do.
A man is not born a master. A master is never proud.
He does not talk down to others.
He is not afraid. He does not tremble.
Nothing binds him. He is infinitely free.
Like water on the leaf of a lotus flower or a mustard seed
on the point of a needle, he does not cling.
He does not tremble or grasp or hesitate.
He has found peace."
　　　　　　　　　– The Dhammapada, "The True Master"[xl]

Mastery is an exquisite state. In mastery, fear of the unknown is finally gone. In mastery, the spirit is in a constant state of wonder and joy. A master knows – the world is not a problem to be solved, but a mystery to be experienced. Every day brings a new adventure. Every adventure is an opportunity to see more, to grow, to give.

Working with the unselfish attitude of service is a fine way to enjoy life. Living according to The Three-Fold Path to Mastery can bring financial success, personal evolution and freedom.

The concepts and suggestions in The Three-Fold Path can be applied to any profession, any industry. The freedom you gain from walking a pathway to mastery comes from within, not just from happiness you derive from the career you've chosen or your relative material success. You can be successful, and be completely bound, stressed out, mean and miserable.

If the guidance in this book can inspire you to make even minor changes in your lifestyle, then you will find that your normal state of mind will become a bit brighter, a bit happier. Strive to follow all the recommendations and you will find that you have not just changed your state of mind – you will have changed your life. From your thoughts, your life is created. As the great mathematician and mystic Blaise Pascal noted, "Man's greatness lies in his power of thought."

Some people immerse themselves in work to the point of collapse, never turning off their cell phones, eating on the run. Other people have the urge to drop everything and run off to a cave in the Himalayas to live a life of reflection and escape the trappings of the worldly life. Neither extreme promises freedom or lasting joy.

The key to a life of mastery is balance. A master doesn't spend 70 hours a week at the office; neither does he spend his entire weekend in lotus position meditating. Both are escapes. Both are unbalanced. Mastery requires the ability to create a life in harmony with the needs of the body, mind and spirit.

The road to mastery requires courage. You may feel at times that you are swimming against the current. Believing in yourself and in the power of your choices, you keep going forward, looking forward, regardless of the masses that may seem to be moving in the opposite direction. This kind of bravery is magnificently portrayed by Gene Kelly in his classic dance scene from "Singin' in the Rain." His character, Don Lockwood, has just bid goodnight to his new love, Kathy Seldon. Rain is coming down in torrents. Gleefully he sends his chauffer away and dances down the street with ecstatic majesty. Cavorting in pools of water, using his umbrella every way but for shelter, he faces a grim policeman and passes other travelers who turn their heads in shock. Here's someone who is drenched, who is walking in the opposite direction from everyone else, and who looks *happy* about it.[xli]

Like Don Lockwood singing and dancing in the rain, travelers on The Three-Fold Path to Mastery don't let other people's choices concern us or temper our glee. We are in love with life, enjoying our path whether it rains or snows or we are bathed in sunlight. We smile at other travelers whether they understand why or not, we work hard, and we keep striving to sing and dance and live and serve as best we can from the bottom of our hearts.

To truly achieve a life of success, fulfillment and joy, consider these thoughts:

Live in the world, but don't be owned by it.

Spend time with other people, but don't lose touch with yourself.

Work hard, then rest.

Give yourself to tasks fully, but find every opportunity to laugh.

Take your work seriously, but not yourself.

When you have become an expert at something, teach others.

There will always be hard days. There will also always be beautiful days.

Remember that no experience is lasting.

Learn from everything. Be grateful for everything.

Spend as much of your energy as possible in service to others. The more you strive to help other people, the less you end up worrying about yourself, and the happier you end up feeling. The moments when you feel least interested in or capable of giving to someone else are often the best times to be generous. By teaching and mentoring, guiding and caring for others, you will increase your own success, your own happiness, your own legacy.

There are no limitations, only obstacles you set for yourself. Believe in whatever beautiful, wondrous, exciting possibilities you want to. Don't hold yourself back by doubt or negativity.

You can become a master if you really want to. It's not impossibly hard if that's where you put your full intent. Life is hard. There will always be some pain and suffering. You might as well work hard and maybe suffer a little in pursuit of becoming a master, because at least mastery will help take away some of the pain. If you are making as much money as you want to, if you are an expert in your field, if you are detached, and if you have given up fear as a way of dealing with the world, you will experience a lot less suffering than the average person.

The most wonderful thing about the path to mastery is the moment when we realize we will never be done. As we work towards one goal or another in life, we seem to always focus on the end point, the final day, the moment when we can look upon our achievement with glory and say that our work is done. Finally, when we reach a level of mastery, we realize we will never be done, and that is even more exciting than thinking there was such a thing as reaching an end. It is like sailing in a boat towards the horizon. Explorers one day realized that the horizon would always be there, that there would never be a point where they would come to the end of the Earth and drop off.

Following The Three-Fold Path to Mastery is like sailing towards a horizon that will never yield a wall. May every reader of this book experience the fulfillment and peace and exultation of reaching mastery, and sailing on.

"Roads go ever ever on..."
– *J.R.R. Tolkien*[xlii]

FOR MORE INFORMATION

For more information about Nicole Grace and Satori Sciences' products, seminars, retreats and offerings, including books and CDs, or to sign up for the free monthly newsletter, please visit our website: http://www.satorisciences.com.

If you would like to share your stories of success using the principles described in *Mastery At Work,* please include your full name, address and phone number and write to us at:

Mastery At Work Success Stories
c/o Satori Sciences, Inc.
369 Montezuma Avenue, Suite 415
Santa Fe, NM 87501
or
feedback@satorisciences.com

We would love to hear from you. We might use your comments in a future product or newsletter, to help inspire someone else on the journey to Mastery.

ACKNOWLEDGEMENTS

I am exceedingly fortunate to have met a qualified spiritual teacher willing to accept me as a student. He always said, "Don't look at me, look at Truth." He encouraged us to revere enlightenment, not to glorify the form of a person. It is easy to encounter my teacher: after an exquisite meditation, when we feel a penetrating sense of peace and can see the light sparkling within all things, there he is. I owe my life and my happiness to his patience, generosity and wisdom. By thanking him I am also thanking everyone whose life has kindly touched my own, since I believe when I see the world, I see his greatness in every particle, every being.

Mastery At Work is dedicated to my dear friend and mentor, Dr. Charles Wurtz. He demonstrates through his every deliberate and impeccable action, and his deeply compassionate heart, the power of a life lived beyond reproach. If ever there were an example of a master, surely he is one.

To Scott Wilson I am eternally grateful. I am constantly in awe of his nobility, integrity and intelligence, as well as his incomparable teaching skills. As President of Satori Sciences he provides the operational and organizational force that has helped make the company a success. In addition, Scott's insightful comments and suggestions throughout my writing of *Mastery At Work* have allowed me to present a far better manuscript than I could ever have done myself.

My family is admirable in their understanding and unconditional support of my less common choices. They have always encouraged my seeking, regardless of how my spiritual journeys strayed from our traditional background. My happiness has always been their primary interest and for that tolerance and love I am truly thankful.

I feel privileged to have trained under gifted martial artists. I am thankful for having had instruction from each of them, in each of their unique styles, and for the discipline they ingrained in me through their commitment to the correct practice of the Warrior Arts.

David Krell and Gary Katz, founders of the International Securities Exchange, give me hope for the future of corporate business. Together they have created one of the most enlightened companies I have ever come across. I am honored to have had the experience of working with them and their brilliant, passionate staff.

The New York City Fire Department Special Operations Command and the City of Santa Fe Fire Department were kind in accepting our offer to train their members in The Three-Fold Path to Mastery through our "Heroes Program." I am overwhelmed by each of these individuals' bravery in choosing firefighting as a career, and I am grateful for their tireless service, which allows the rest of us to live more safely.

To Linda I offer deepest thanks for taking such good care of me. I am fortunate to have you in my life.

I humbly thank each of my students for teaching me more about life and the Path than I could have ever learned without you. Thank you for giving me the opportunity to evolve with you, and to share with you that which I love most.

I have been blessed with extraordinary teachers and mentors, whose wisdom and instruction are exemplary. Any errors in this book are entirely my own.

ABOUT THE AUTHOR

Nicole Grace is Founder and Chief Executive Officer of Satori Sciences, Inc., a personal and professional development corporation specializing in teaching her Three-Fold Path to Mastery philosophy, an enlightened approach to life and work. An ordained Buddhist monk, Nicole Grace is also a nationally respected teacher of meditation and spirituality, an accomplished violinist and a black belt in karate. She offers *Mastery At Work* and meditation seminars and retreats, as well as private coaching and motivational presentations on how to apply the highest and noblest principles to achieving success, fulfillment and joy in life and work.

ENDNOTES

[i] A version of this tale can be found in the book by Swami Prabhavananda. *The Eternal Companion: Brahmananda, His Life and Teachings.* Hollywood: Vedanta Press, 1970. Page 63. This well-known story can also be found in several other sources.

[ii] Regardie, Israel. *The Tree of Life: A Study in Magic.* York Beach, Maine: Samuel Weiser, Inc., 1972. Page 234.

[iii] *Ace Ventura: When Nature Calls.* Directed by Steve Oedekerk. With Jim Carrey. Warner Brothers, 1995.

[iv] Holmes, T. & Rahe, R. "Holmes-Rahe Social Readjustment Rating Scale." *Journal of Psychosomatic Research,* vol. II, 1967.

[v] Swami Rama Tirtha. "The Way to the Fulfilment of All Desires." Lecture to the Hermetic Brotherhood. United States, December 13, 1902.

[vi] Winfrey, Oprah. Interview, *Academy of Achievement.* http://www.achievement.org. 1991.

[vii] Peter Jensen, PhD, "The Role of Imagery in Mental Preparation." *The Atlantis Newsletter,* http://www.imagerynet.com/atlantis.

[viii] "Short tenure: O'Leary out at Notre Dame after one week." *Sports Illustrated* online edition. http://sportsillustrated.cnn.com. December 14, 2001.

[ix] Swami Prabhavananda. *The Eternal Companion: Brahmananda, His Life and Teachings.* Hollywood: Vedanta Society of Southern California, 1970. Page 24.

[x] Ramana Maharshi. *The Spiritual Teaching of Ramana Maharshi.* Foreward by C.G. Jung. Boston: Shambhala Publications, 1988.

[xi] Packard, David. *The HP Way: How Bill Hewlett and I Built Our Company.* New York: Harper Business, 1996.

[xii] *Ramayana.* Retold by William Buck. Berkeley: University of California Press, 2000. Page 426.

[xiii] There are many sources for the Seven Virtues representing the Bushido Code, though translations from the Japanese into English vary slightly. For a good reference on these principles, see: Nitobe, Inazo. *Bushido: The Warrior's Code.* Burbank: Ohara Publications, Incorporated, 1979.

[xiv] *Chushingura: The Treasury of Loyal Retainers.* Translated by Donald Keene. New York: Columbia University Press, 1997.

[xv] Nitobe, Inazo. *Bushido: Samurai Ethics and the Soul of Japan.* Mineola, New York: Dover Publications, 2004.

[xvi] "2003 Year in Review." Venture Reporter. Dow Jones and Company, Inc., 2004.

[xvii] Suzuki, Shunryu. *Zen Mind, Beginner's Mind: Informal Talks on Zen Meditation and Practice.* New York: Weatherhill, 1977.

[xviii] For a version of this well-known Zen story, see: *Zen Flesh, Zen Bones: A Collection of Zen and Pre-Zen Writings.* Compiled by Paul Reps and Nyogen Senzaki. Boston: Shambhala Publications, 1994.

[xix] "Katha." *The Upanishads: Breath of the Eternal.* The Principle Texts Selected and Translated from the Original Sanskrit by Swami Prabhavananda and Frederick Manchester. New York: Mentor, 1975.

[xx] Musashi, Miyamoto. "The Water Scroll." *The Book of Five Rings.* Translated by Thomas Cleary. Boston: Shambhala, 1994.

[xxi] Tzu, Sun. *The Art of War.* Translated by Thomas Cleary. Boston: Shambhala Publications, 1991.

[xxii] Swami Nikhilananda. *Holy Mother: Being the Life of Sri Sarada Devi, Wife of Sri Ramakrishna and Helpmate in His Mission.* New York: Ramakrishna-Vivekenanda Center, 1997. Pages 93 and 103.

[xxiii] "Mind." *Dhammapada: The Sayings of the Buddha.* Rendered by Thomas Byrom. Boston: Shambhala Publications, 1976.

[xxiv] Allen, James. *As A Man Thinketh.* New York: Barnes & Noble Books, 1992.

xxv Frost, Robert. "The Road Not Taken." *The Road Not Taken and Other Poems*. Mineola, NY: Dover Publications, Inc. 1993.

xxvi Guru Rinpoche. "The Main Verses of the Six Bardos." *The Tibetan Book of the Dead: The Great Liberation Through Hearing in the Bardo*. Translated by Francesca Fremantle and Chogyam Trungpa, Boston: Shambhala Publications, 1992.

xxvii Homer. *The Odyssey (Collector's Library)*. Translated by T.E. Lawrence. New York: Barnes & Noble Books, 2004. Page 213.

xxviii For a book about this phenomenon see: Murphy, Michael and White, Rhea. *Into the Zone: Transcendent Experience in Sports*. New York: Penguin, 1995 (updated from the original version published in 1978).

xxix *Shine*. Directed by Scott Hicks. With Geoffrey Rush and Noah Taylor. Fine Line Features, 1996.

xxx Tzu, Sun. "Planning A Siege." *The Art of War*. Translated by Thomas Cleary. Boston: Shambhala Publications, 1988.

xxxi Young, John H. *A Guide to the Manners, Etiquette, and Deportment of the Most Refined Society*. Guilford, Connecticut: The Lyons Press, 2001.

xxxii Carnegie, Dale. *How to Win Friends & Influence People*. New York: Simon & Schuster Adult Publishing Group, 1982.

xxxiii Homer. *The Odyssey (Collector's Library)*. Translated by T.E. Lawrence. New York: Barnes & Noble Books, 2004.

xxxiv I heard this story from a wise and funny Buddhist teacher. I have not found it published in any text.

xxxv Carnegie, Dale. *How to Win Friends & Influence People*. New York: Simon & Schuster Adult Publishing Group, 1982.

xxxvi Mullin, Glen. *Path of the Bodhisattva Warrior: The Life and Teachings of the Thirteenth Dalai Lama*. Wheaton, Illinois: Snow Lion Publications, 1987.

xxxvii "Choices." *Dhammapada: The Sayings of the Buddha*. Rendered by Thomas Byrom. Boston: Shambhala Publications, 1976.

xxxviii For a mystical description of *stalking,* see: Castaneda, Carlos. *The Power of Silence: Further Lessons of Don Juan*. New York: Washington Square Press, 1987.

[xxxix] I came across this "study" on the internet. Although I found close to fifty sites posting this information, I was not able to find the original source. Due to its considerable reproduction online, I am treating the contents of the study as "in the public domain."

[xl] "The True Master." *Dhammapada: The Sayings of the Buddha*. Rendered by Thomas Byrom. Boston: Shambhala Publications, 1976.

[xli] *Singin' in the Rain*. Directed by Stanley Donen. With Gene Kelly and Debbie Reynolds. MGM, 1952.

[xlii] Tolkien, J.R.R. *The Hobbit*. Boston: Houghton Mifflin Company, 1938.